Délices Créoles

DESSERTS

DÉLICES CRÉOLES

DESSERTS

EXOTIC DESSERTS FROM THE FRENCH CARIBBEAN

KÖNEMANN

Acknowledgments

Level of difficulty of the recipes:

★   easy
★★   advanced
★★★   challenging

Original edition 1997 © Fabien Bellahsen und Daniel Rouche
Photos: Studio Lucien Loeb/Didier Bizos
Original title: Délices des Îles - Desserts individuels

Recipe Coordinator:
Jean Bordier
Meilleur ouvrier de France, Président d'Honneur de l'Association des Maîtres Cuisiniers de France, Membre titulaire de l'Académie Culinaire de France, Chevalier de l'Ordre National du Mérite, Officier du Mérite agricole

Chefs and Pastry Chefs:
Michel Comby
Maître Cuisinier de France, Membre titulaire de l'Académie Culinaire de France, Officier du Mérite agricole, Vainqueur du 1er Trophée Taittinger
Alain Nonnet
Maître Cuisinier de France, Membre titulaire de l'Académie Culinaire de France, Chevalier de l'Ordre National du Mérite, Officier du Mérite agricole
Frank Saksik: Chef-Pâtissier
Olivier Garrivet: Assistant-Pâtissier

Copyright © 1999 for the English edition
Könemann Verlagsgesellschaft mbH
Bonner Straße 126, D-50968 Cologne

Translation from French: Mary Margaret Chappell
English-language editor: Sally Schreiber
Coordination and typesetting: Agents - Producers - Editors, Overath
Reproduction: Reproservice Werner Pees, Essen
Production manager: Detlev Schaper
Printing and binding: Leefung Asco Printers Ltd., Hong Kong

Printed in China

ISBN 3-8290-2762-1

10 9 8 7 6 5 4 3 2 1

Contents

Foreword

The arts of cooking, baking, and confection-making have always played an integral role in festive occasions the world over, and are an especially important part of French cultural heritage. In recent years the interest in less familiar regions and their culinary traditions has grown. The series *Délices Créole: Exotic Desserts from the French Caribbean* is dedicated to the sweet delicacies of that distant island paradise. The three volumes—Desserts, Cakes, and Confections—reveal a wide array of new and exotic recipes.

Renowned chefs, pastry chefs and confectioners from France and the French territories in the Antilles invite you to discover the delicious possibilities offered by the wide variety of island produce available today. They would like you to explore their culinary world, in which luscious fresh fruits and fragrant spices form the basis of recipes as surprising aas they are succulent. Readily available tropical fruits such as kiwi, pineapples, oranges and melons, as well as lesser-known types such as mangos, carambolas (or star fruits), kumquats and guavas, are used in most of the recipes. These experts have created subtle, daring and sometimes unexpected combinations which are sure to inspire your imagination and teach you something new about the possibilities of marrying taste, color, flavor and fragrance.

Even local products take on a surprisingly exotic flavor when combined with ingredients like curry and cardamom, ginger and aniseed, coconut and rum. From simple sweets to refined delicacies that will delight even the most finicky gourmet, these recipes conjure up images of warm sunshine, sandy beaches, and palm trees.

This collection of recipes takes you on a culinary journey to an exotic island paradise full of vibrant colors, aromas, and fragrances. The detailed step-by-step instructions and color photographs make it easy for you to try the recipes on your own. Suggestions for substitutions and variations in flavors are provided along with the recipes, so your efforts are sure to be successful. In addition, each recipe is accompanied by an informative text describing the culture and tradition of the region or the historical background of a recipe and the origin of its ingredients.

The chefs hope that they have been able to convey their love of their craft in the volumes of this series. Allow yourself to be carried away to the sensuous pleasures of the islands, and spoil your family and guests with some of the finest delicacies paradise has to offer.

Bon appétit!

Crispy Pineapple Napoleon

1 pineapple
4½ oz/125 g pastry cream (see basic recipe)
6½ tbsp/100 ml whipped cream
1 cinnamon stick, freshly ground
2 custard apples
2 cups/500 ml sugar syrup (see basic recipe)

Serves 4
Preparation time: 20 minutes
Cooking time: 4 hours 20 minutes
Chilling time: 1 hour
Difficulty: ★

The skin of the custard apple has a beautiful scaly texture. Its white flesh is slightly tough and is more frequently used in compotes once the black seeds have been entirely removed. The floral flavor of the custard apple resembles that of a pear, and is enhanced by the cinnamon spice. The clear, aromatic taste of the two combine exceptionally well with the slightly caramelized flavor of the pineapple.

In preparing this dessert, it is important to dry the thin slices of pineapple well. The slices should be cut with a very long, sharp knife. Once the slices have been candied and baked, remove them from the baking sheet while still hot. Allow them to harden on a separate piece of parchment paper dusted with confectioners' sugar to keep them from sticking together.

To assemble the dessert, fan out three pineapple slices on a clean workspace: Lay down one slice of pineapple, cover it with the custard apple cream then repeat. Finish by placing a third pineapple slice on top.

Place the finished crispy pineapple fan on the plate. Decorate the plate by alternating several custard apple seeds with dots of fruit coulis. This coulis may be prepared by blending persimmons or other fruit with sugar syrup until smooth. Serve immediately while the pineapple slices are crispy.

1. Cut the pineapple into very fine slices. Place the slices in a saucepan, cover with the syrup and boil for 20 minutes to candy them.

2. Remove the pineapple slices from the syrup and place them on a baking sheet lined with parchment paper to dry. Cover the slices with a second sheet of parchment. Place a second baking sheet on top for weight. Bake 4 hours at 200 °F/90 °C.

with Custard Apples

3. Peel the custard apples and cut into quarters. Remove the black seeds and reserve them as garnish. Chop the custard apple quarters into small pieces.

4. To make the custard apple cream, mix together the pastry cream, ground cinnamon and the chopped custard apple. Gently incorporate the whipped cream. Carefully spread a spoonful of the cream onto a pineapple slice. Place a second slice of pineapple on top and repeat. Finish with a third pineapple slice. Garnish and serve.

1 small pineapple
1 cup/250 ml water
1 cup/250 g sugar
juice of one lemon
mint leaves

Spun sugar garnish:
1 cup/250 g sugar
⅓ cup/80 ml water

Frosty

Serves   4
Preparation time: 25 minutes
Cooking time: 10 minutes
Freezing time: 1 hour
Difficulty: ★

Discovered by European explorers in Brazil during the 16th century, the pineapple was first introduced in England and later cultivated in France during the reign of Louis XV. A delicacy in colonial America, the pineapple came to symbolize hospitality and was used to decorate houses for the Christmas holidays. This dessert is inspired by fresh pineapple sorbets served in the French Antilles, where the pineapple is called the king of fruits.

For this recipe, select a small pineapple which is sweet, full of flavor and not too stringy. Blend the pulp of the pineapple to perfect smoothness. Prepare the sugar syrup. If it seems too sweet, it can be lightened with a bit of water or lemon juice, but if you lack an ice cream maker to turn the sorbet, you may buy pineapple sorbet to fill the pineapple shell.

The mint leaves used to garnish the pineapple may be replaced by verbena or a frosted branch of rosemary. Other pulp fruits such as grapefruit, orange, lemon or lime can be employed in this recipe as well. The sorbet recipes you choose to try may also be flavored with rum, vanilla extract or other alcohols and flavors.

The golden threads of spun sugar which decorate this dessert are made by drawing fine threads of hot caramel over aluminum foil using two forks. Dip the forks into the caramel and wave them over the aluminum foil surface. Once the spun sugar has cooled, it comes off the foil easily and can be used to decorate the pineapple.

1. Cut open the pineapple and carefully scoop out the pulp without damaging the skin. Reserve the pineapple shell. Prepare the sugar syrup by boiling the sugar and water together at 250 °F/120 °C for 10 minutes.

2. Blend the pinapple pulp till smooth. Add the lemon juice and syrup..

Pineapple Sorbet

3. Taste the pineapple mixture. If it is too sweet, add water as necessary to balance the taste. Pour the mixture into an ice cream maker.

4. Freeze the pineapple sorbet for 1 hour. Scoop the pineapple sorbet and fill the reserved pineapple shell. Decorate with mint leaves and spun sugar. Spun sugar is made by using 2 forks to draw thin threads of caramelized sugar across a foil-covered surface.

Exotic Fresh

½ mango
2 kiwis
4 gooseberries
1 banana
½ pineapple
½ pomegranate
2 passionfruits
2 clementines
2 prickly pears
1 star fruit
4 mangosteens
½ watermelon

For the fruit coulis:
1 cup/250 ml sugar syrup (see
    basic recipe)
3½ tbsp/50 ml rum

For the avocado cream:
1 avocado
zest and juice of ½ lemon
3½ tbsp/50 ml white rum
1 cup/250 ml heavy cream
2 tbsp/30 g sugar

Serves   4
Preparation time: 30 minutes
Difficulty: ★

In creating this festival of exotic fruits, our chef wanted to celebrate the wide variety of tastes and sensations to be found in exotic fruits: sweet, sour and peppery flavors. All of the fruits in this recipe are used raw without the addition of sugar. When using this recipe, feel free to explore and expand on it, according to your own preferences and tastes. The list of fruits given in the ingredients is just a small example of the exotic fruits that can be found on the market. Papayas, guavas, persimmons, etc. also make excellent additions to the presentation.

Chef's hint: Use knives with long, very sharp blades in order to cut the fruit as cleanly as possible. Once the fruit has been sliced, arrange it around a large, preferably dark plate to show off the wide variety of colors.

The success of this exotic fruit plate lies in its garnish. Make a colorful fruit coulis made according to your palate: Blend leftover fruit pieces (except for the star fruit and kiwi) and add sugar syrup to obtain the desired consistency.

The avocado cream and smooth fruit coulis which are served with the fruits in this dessert are the ideal accompaniment for the fresh fruit. We suggest dipping the fruit slices in the avocado cream then into the smooth fruit coulis to bring out the natural flavors of the fruit.

1. Slice all fruit except the watermelon with a very sharp knife. Scoop the watermelon into balls using a melon baller. Select the most regular slices of fruit for the plate; set aside all ends or leftover bits to be used in the fruit coulis.

2. Peel the avocado and cut in half. Remove the pit and press the avocado through a sieve using a scraper. Add the lemon juice and zest along with the rum. In a separate bowl, whip the heavy cream with the sugar. Fold the whipped cream into the avocado mixture.

Fruit Plate

3. To make the fruit coulis, blend the leftover bits of fruit until smooth. Add the rum and the sugar syrup. Chill.

4. Using the avocado cream and the fruit coulis as a centerpiece, arrange the sliced fruit on individual serving plates.

Saint Anne Filled Crêpes

For the crêpe batter:
1 cup/120 g flour
3 eggs
2 tbsp sugar
3½ tbsp/50 ml dark rum
1 vanilla bean, scraped
1⅔ cup/400 ml milk
6½ tbsp/100 ml heavy cream
2 tsp/10 g brown butter (see basic recipe)

For the fruit filling:
2 bananas, cubed
¼ pineapple, cubed
1 cup/150 g dried fruit, chopped
4 tsp/20 g butter, melted

Serves	*4*
Preparation time:	*35 minutes*
Cooking time:	*25 minutes*
Refrigeration time:	*2 hours*
Difficulty:	★

For the coffee custard:
6 egg yolks
6½ tbsp/100 g sugar
1½ cups/350 ml milk
¼ cup espresso or very strong coffee
1 vanilla bean

For the garnish:
chopped pistachios and almonds

The batter should rest several hours before you make the crêpes to allow the gluten in the flour to develop and improve the consistency of the crêpes. Our chef recommends that you make the crêpes thinner than usual so that they will be easier to shape and tie. The crêpe batter has been flavored with rum and vanilla which bring out the flavors of the dried fruit.

In electing the dried fruit for this recipe, we have chosen dried apricots, candied kumquats, almonds, peanuts and green pistachios. Other fruits and nuts may be substituted according to taste and availability. The fruit and nuts may be roasted several minutes in the oven to soften the fruits and enhance their flavor.

When making the coffee custard, stir the mixture continually over low heat to keep the yolks from coagulating and creating lumps. Strain the custard and serve it hot or cold, sprinkled with chopped pistachios and almonds. The flavor of the custard may be varied to vanilla, orange or cinnamon using the same basic custard recipe given here.

In preparing the dessert, we have tied up the crêpe purses with the vanilla beans used to flavor the crêpe batter and sauce, but you may also close the crêpe with a small toothpick to hold the purse in place.

1. Prepare the crêpe batter. Mix all of the ingredients in the order given, adding the brown butter last. Let the batter rest for 2 hours or more in the refrigerator. Remove the vanilla bean and reserve. Cook the crêpes in a lightly buttered pan for 3 minutes on each side.

2. To make the filling, stir together the dried fruit, bananas, pineapple and butter.

with Coffee Custard

3. Fill the crêpes with the fruit (approximately 2 tablespoons of filling per crêpe). To make the coffee custard, whisk together the egg yolks and sugar. In a saucepan, bring the milk and coffee to a boil with the vanilla bean. Whisk the milk into the yolk mixture. Remove the vanilla bean and reserve. Return the custard to the saucepan. Poach the custard for 2 to 3 minutes over low heat.

4. Tie up the crêpes into a purse using the leftover vanilla beans which have been halved lengthwise. Coat the bottom of the plate with the coffee custard. Sprinkle with chopped almonds or pistachios and place the crêpe in the center.

Tradewind

For the baba dough:
¼ cup warm water
1 scant tbsp/12 g yeast
2 cups/250 g flour
3 eggs
a pinch of salt
1 tbsp/15 g sugar
6 tbsp/90 g butter, softened

For the passion fruit cream:
2 passion fruit
4 tsp/20 g sugar
2 cups/500 ml heavy cream
3½ tbsp/50 ml white rum

For the soaking liquid:
1 quart/1 liter sugar syrup (see
  basic recipe)
¾ cup/200 ml dark rum

For the garnish:
2 slices pineapple
mint leaves

Serves	4
Preparation time:	40 minutes
Cooking time:	20 minutes
Rising time:	1 hour
Difficulty:	0★ ★

The baba dessert is of Polish origin. In Polish, a *babka* is an old woman with a pot belly—and indeed, the dessert resembles the shape of an old woman. King Stanislas Leczinsky of Poland, then Duke of Lorraine, is credited with introducing the dessert to France where it is now considered to be a traditional French pastry. Leczinsky changed the name of the dessert from *babka* to *baba* so that it would have the same name as Ali Baba, his favorite hero from the *Thousand and One Nights*.

Certain steps are essential to the success of this dessert: The flour must be sifted well to avoid lumps in the dough, the yeast must be fresh and therefore still active, and an aged, dark rum full of flavor must be used to in the soaking liquid for the babas.

Make sure that all the ingredients for the baba dough are at room temperature so that the dough will be neither too firm nor too runny. Using a pastry bag, fill the baba pans to the top: the dough will double in size and rise over the edge of the molds during baking. If you do not have small individual baba pans, a larger tube pan or bundt pan may also be used. Bake the larger baba for 30 minutes at 375 °F/190 °C.

To decorate the baba, cut the pineapple slices into triangles. Stick the points of the triangles into the passion fruit cream and top the dessert with a sprig of mint. Serve with hot tea, coffee or a glass of fruit liqueur.

1. Dissolve the yeast in ¼ cup warm water. Stir in ½ cup of flour. Add the rest of the flour, the eggs, a pinch of salt and the sugar. Beat the dough until silky smooth. Let the dough rise for 1 hour in a warm place. Beat in the softened butter.

2. Using a pastry bag, pipe the dough into buttered baba pans. Bake at 400 °F/200 °C for 20 minutes.

Baba au Rhum

3. Unmold the babas and allow them to cool. Bring the sugar syrup to a boil. Away from the heat, add the rum. Dip each baba into the hot rum and sugar syrup mixture and allow it to absorb as much liquid as possible. Place the babas on a rack or a sheet of parchment paper to drain any excess syrup.

4. Scoop out the centers of the passion fruit. Mix the pulp with the white rum. Fold in the whipped cream. Pipe this cream into the center of the babas. Decorate with mint and pineapple and serve chilled.

Ginger-Roasted

12 baby bananas
1½ oz/40 g fresh ginger, grated
2 tbsp/30 g butter
2 tbsp plus 1 tsp/50 g honey
½ cup (generous)/70 g slivered almonds

For the ginger sauce:
6½ tbsp/100 ml coconut milk
¾ cup/200 ml banana juice
a pinch of ground ginger

Serves	4
Preparation time:	15 minutes
Cooking time:	10 minutes
Difficulty:	★

The ginger root, cultivated and widely used in warm climates around the globe, is both pungent and spicy hot. We have chosen the bold taste of fresh ginger along with the milder ground ginger to bring out the subtle flavors of the honey and the bananas in this recipe. Our chef has added a few drops of dark rum to the ginger sauce to further enhance the flavor.

When selecting fresh ginger for this recipe, choose roots with smooth, firm skin, not those that look soft or wrinkled. Select baby bananas which are firm to the touch and whose flesh is thick but not hard. Firmer bananas hold their shape and flavor better when roasted.

For the caramel, honey or sugar may be used with or without butter. Allow the caramel to take on a light amber color before adding the bananas. Baby bananas cook more quickly than mature ones, and may therefore be roasted whole. Once the bananas are cooked though and thoroughly coated with the caramel, place them on the plate, surround them with the sauce and serve piping hot.

Variations on the roasted, caramelized fruit dessert presented here call for pineapple or papaya slices in the place of the bananas, and walnuts or pine nuts instead of slivered almonds.

1. Carefully peel the baby bananas without breaking them. Peel and grate the ginger.

2. In a frying pan, cook the honey and butter to a caramel. When it begins to brown, add the bananas and sauté them on each side until golden brown.

Baby Bananas

3. Add the grated ginger and the slivered almonds to the hot caramel. Cook a few minutes longer until the almonds begin to brown.

4. Whisk the coconut milk, banana juice and the ground ginger together in a bowl. Heat this sauce without bringing it to a boil. Place the roasted bananas and almonds on the plate and garnish with the ginger sauce.

Carnival Beignets

For the beignet dough:
¾ cup/200 ml milk
1½ oz/40 g yeast
5 cups/600 g flour
1 tsp/5 g salt
4 eggs
2 tsp/10 g sugar
⅓ cup/80 g butter
¾ cup/200 ml rum

For the sweet potato filling:
3 sweet potatoes, peeled and diced
6½ tbsp/100 g brown sugar
1 whole nutmeg, grated

For the garnish:
confectioners' sugar

Serves	4
Preparation time:	35 minutes
Cooking time:	40 minutes
Rising time:	40 minutes
Difficulty:	★ ★

The splendor of Carnival in the French Antilles is renowned throughout the world. It is the most popular celebration in the region and ends on Mardi Gras, with the burning of the *Vaval*.

During the festivities of Carnival, when excess becomes the norm, gastronomic delights are de rigueur, and d. desserts hold a special place in the celebration. Fantastic creations abound as cooks and chefs alike give free reign to their imagination. Our chef has chosen to incorporate sweet potatoes,which are indigenous to the Antilles, in our version of Carnival beignets.

It is very important to make the beignet dough light enough to float on top of the hot oil (or lard) so that it will cook evenly to a golden brown. Passion fruit liqueur may be substituted for the rum as flavoring for the beignet dough. Lemon or lime zest can be added to the sweet potato filling to enhance the flavor. Other fillings such as homemade jams or pastry cream may also be used instead of the sweet potato filling here.

Drain the beignets well before serving and sprinkle with confectioners' sugar and serve hot.

1. For the sweet potato filling, combine the brown sugar and diced sweet potatoes, the grate the nutmeg over the mixture. Cook until lightly caramelized and soft enough to mash. Blend the filling until smooth. Make a yeast starter for the beignet dough by dissolving the yeast in ½ cup milk and stirring in 1¼ cups flour. Cover the starter and let it rise for 30 minutes in a warm place.

2. In a saucepan, whisk the eggs with the sugar over low heat. Continue to whisk and poach the mixture for 10 minutes. Place the yeast starter in the bowl of a mixer and add the salt, and the rest of the flour and milk. Beat in the cooked egg and sugar mixture, the softened butter and the rum. Continue to beat the dough until it pulls away from the sides of the bowl. Allow the dough to rest for 10 minutes.

with Sweet Potato Filling

3. Fill a saucepan with 1½ inches of oil and heat to 355 °F/180 °C. Shape the beignets into circles and drop them into the oil. Cook for approximately 5 minutes on each side, flipping them from time to time to cook uniformly. Drain the beignets on paper towels.

4. Using a small pastry tip, pierce the top of the beignets and pipe the sweet potato filling into them. Sprinkle with confectioners' sugar and serve hot.

Spice Cake with

For the spice cake:
4 eggs
6½ tbsp/100 g brown sugar
a pinch of cinnamon
a pinch of ground cloves
6½ tbsp/50 g whole wheat flour
1 tbsp/15 g cornstarch

For the marmalade:
6½ tbsp/100 g brown sugar
1 orange
1 mango
1 star fruit
a pinch of nutmeg

Serves   4
Preparation time: 30 minutes
Cooking time: 1 hour 10 minutes
Difficulty: ★

This basic spice cake recipe is simple yet delicious. It is mildly sweet and makes an excellent accompaniment to brunch fare or afternoon tea. The cinnamon and cloves used here may be replaced by other spices such as ground coriander and curry powder. The cake is done when it pulls away from the sides of the pan and a knife inserted in the center of the cake comes out clean. This cake will keep for several days wrapped in plastic wrap in the refrigerator. Select fruit with firm flesh for the marmalade so that the fruit remains intact when cooked. Guavas, papayas or bananas are also suitable for this recipe.

Although this dessert is relatively simple to prepare, much of its success depends upon the oven temperature at which it is baked. Preheating the oven is essential for best results: The cake should begin baking the moment it is put in the oven. Place the cake pan on a shelf in the middle of the oven so that the oven heat surrounds it evenly. Avoid opening the oven too often; frequent changes in oven temperature will keep the cake from baking evenly.

1. Separate the eggs. Whisk the yolks with the brown sugar. Add the cinnamon and cloves. Using a spatula or wooden spoon, stir in the flour and the cornstarch.

2. In a separate bowl, beat the egg whites to stiff peaks. Fold the egg whites into the yolk mixture.

Tropical Fruit Marmalade

3. Butter 4 individual round cake pans and fill them with the spice cake batter using a spoon. Bake for 45 minutes in a 350 °F/180 °C oven or until the cakes begin to pull away from the sides of the pan. Cool the spice cakes in the pans and unmold.

4. To prepare the marmalade, cut the orange, the star fruit and the mango into small cubes. Cook the fruit, brown sugar and nutmeg in a sauté pan over low heat for 25 minutes, stirring regularly.

Chocolate Charlotte

For the sponge cake:
3 eggs
1 cup/250 ml water
½ cup/130 g sugar
1 cup/130 g flour
¼ tsp/5 g baking powder
3 tbsp/30 g cocoa powder

For the chocolate mousse:
6¼ oz/155 g high quality dark chocolate
⅔ cup/150 ml heavy cream, whipped

For the coconut-curry sabayon:
1 cup/250 ml coconut milk
4 egg yolks
8 tsp sugar
a pinch of curry powder
3½ tbsp/50 ml white rum

For the garnish:
1 cup (generous)/100 g freshly
   grated coconut
1¾ oz/50 g high quality dark
   chocolate, melted

Serves   4
Preparation time: 1 hour 30 minutes
Cooking time: 30 minutes
Refrigeration time: 30 minutes
Difficulty: ★ ★ ★

While yellow curry powder is usually associated with Asian and Indian cooking, it is also widely used in the Caribbean islands in both sweet and savory recipes. Curry goes very well with the light creamy flavor of coconut. We have chosen to garnish our chocolate charlotte with fresh coconut and a curry sabayon made with coconut milk. If fresh coconut is not available, dried coconut may be used. Our chef uses fresh coconut which he roasts a few minutes in the oven to bring out its flavor.

When adding the coconut milk to the sabayon mixture, check that the mixture is warm to the touch, not hot. Continue cooking over low heat, whisking to obtain a light airy mousse. Once the sauce is of the right consistency, flavor it with the curry and rum or substitute cinnamon or vanilla extract for a different variety.

Dark bittersweet chocolate is the ideal complement to the coconut and curry in this recipe. We recommend a strong bittersweet chocolate with a 70% cocoa content. Certain conditions must be respected when using dark chocolate: it must be completely melted when mixed with the whipped cream. This dessert must be chilled before serving to allow the sponge cake to absorb the flavors of the chocolate mousse and the coconut—but be sure to keep the dessert covered until serving time to protect the sponge cake from absorbing odors.

1. Whisk together the ingredients for the sponge cake, adding the cocoa powder last. Spread the batter evenly (⅛ inch/2 mm) onto a piece of parchment paper. Bake at 430 °F/220 °C for 4 to 5 minutes or until the cake springs back to the touch.

2. Melt the chocolate in a stainless steel bowl over a pot of boiling water (or use a double boiler), stirring constantly. When all the chocolate has melted but not yet become hot, fold in the whipped cream with a spatula.

with Coconut-Curry Sauce

3. Bring the coconut milk to a boil. Heat the yolks and the sugar over low heat and beat to ribbon consistency. Pour the coconut milk over the yolk mixture, whisking constantly. Cook the mixture gently over low heat until it becomes a thick mousse, then stir in the curry and rum.

4. Cut the chocolate sponge cake into strips sufficiently long and wide to line a cake ring. Fill the circle to the top with chocolate mousse, sprinkle with freshly grated coconut, and chill for 30 minutes. Serve with the coconut-curry sauce and melted dark chocolate as garnish.

Golden

For the blini batter:
2 tbsp/25 g yeast
1 cup/250 ml milk
a pinch of sugar
6½ tbsp/50 g all-purpose flour
1¼ cups/150 g whole wheat flour
2 egg yolks
3 egg whites

For the pomegranate cream:
1 pomegranate
½ cup/125 ml sugar syrup (see
   basic recipe)

1 sheet gelatin
⅔ cup/150 ml heavy cream
1 tbsp/30 g confectioners' sugar

For the fruit center:
4½ oz/125 g strawberries
2 kiwis
1 mango
1 pink grapefruit

Serves	4
Preparation time:	35 minutes
Cooking time:	6 minutes per blini
Rising time:	1 hour
Difficulty:	★ ★

Blinis or blintzes are small round Russian pancakes traditionally served with sour cream and butter as hors d'oeuvres. Special blini pans are about 7 inches/15 cm in diameter with high sides and a thick cast-iron bottom to insure even cooking.

Although blinis are usually made with white and buckwheat flours, our chef has chosen wholewheat flour for a lighter, more delicately-flavored pancake. Because all of the wheat grain is used in whole wheat flour, we recommend organic whole wheat flour, which is free of pesticides and fertilizers that can remain on the outer shell of the wheat grain.

Select a variety of brightly colored fruits to fill the blinis: Here, we have used green kiwi, orange mango, red strawberry and pink grapefruit. Cut the first three fruits into fine slices. Cut sections from the grapefruit to remove the pith and seeds.

The grenadine (pomegranate syrup) is made by boiling the pomegranate seeds with the sugar syrup then blending the mixture to a smooth pulp. If fresh pomegranates are not available, commercial grenadine syrup may be used in both the cream and the garnish of this dessert.

To assemble the dessert, place a blini in the center of the plate. Pipe or spoon the grenadine cream onto the blini. Alternating colors, spread the sliced fruit in a fan over the cream and cover with a second blini, allowing the fruit to show on one side. Garnish the plate with a crescent of grenadine syrup.

1. To prepare the blini batter, dissolve the yeast in the warm milk. Add a pinch of sugar, the flours and the egg yolks. In a separate bowl, whip the egg whites until they form soft peaks. Fold the egg whites into the yeast mixture. Let the batter rise in a warm place for 1 hour.

2. Lightly butter a blini pan. Ladle the risen blini batter into the pan and cook over low heat for 3 minutes on each side.

Caribbean Blinis

3. To make the grenadine, bring the pomegranate seeds to a boil with the sugar syrup. Blend the syrup and seeds until smooth. Soften the gelatin sheet in cold water, drain it and add it to the grenadine syrup. Allow the syrup to cool.

4. Whip the cream until it forms soft peaks, then beat in the confectioners' sugar. Fold in the grenadine and gelatin mixture with a rubber spatula. Pipe or spoon the cream onto the blini, and place the sliced fruit on top of the cream, alternating colors. Cover with a second blini cocked slightly to the side to show off the colors of the fruit.

Crispy Feuilles de Brick

1 package *feuilles de brick*
3 tbsp/50 g butter

For the exotic fruit marmalade:
1 star fruit
½ pineapple
1 persimmon
¾ cup plus 1 tbsp/200 g sugar

For the frangipani filling:
7 tbsp/50 g almond flour
3 tbsp/50 g sugar
3 tbsp/50 g butter, softened

For the honey sauce:
1 tbsp/20 g honey
1 cup/250 ml orange juice
several saffron stigmas

Serves	*4*
Preparation time:	*1 hour*
Cooking time:	*45 minutes*
Difficulty:	★ ★

Feuille de brick is the French name for a paper-thin crêpe made using semolina flour. The semolina is boiled down with water to make a consistent batter which is cooked on a griddle greased with olive oil. Traditionally, the feuille de brick is prepared by hand and requires patience and dexterity. The batter is spread onto the hot griddle with the bare hand dipped in cold water, and the thin crêpe is simultaneously loosened from the griddle with a knife. The feuille de brick is then placed on a dry towel to cool. Ready-made feuilles de brick can be found in the frozen foods section of gourmet stores, or you may use regular crêpes for this recipe.

The hardest part of this recipe is folding the feuilles de brick into triangles. Cut the feuille de brick in half and fold it into a cone to envelop the marmalade and the frangipani filling. Turn the feuille de brick so that the point of the cone points upward. Repeat the process using the rounded side of the feuille de brick: Fold the sides over to make a second triangular cone, then fold the second triangle over the first to form one thick triangle. Place a small pat of butter on the triangles and brown the feuilles de brick in the oven for 15 minutes at 350 °F/180 °C to give them a light, crunchy texture.

A honey sauce or a warm fruit coulis may be used to garnish the plate along with candied orange zest, but other exotic fruits may be used in this dessert as well, such as mangos, papayas and pineapple.

1. To prepare the marmalade, dice the fruit and mix well with the sugar. Simmer ½ hour over low heat until the syrup becomes thick but the bits of fruit remain intact.

2. Prepare the frangipani filling by beating the softened butter with the almond flour and the sugar. Cut the feuilles de brick in half with a sharp knife, taking care not to tear them.

with Exotic Fruit Marmalade

3. With the straight edge of the cut feuille toward you, place a spoonful each of marmalade and the frangipani filling on the left side of it. Fold into a cone, then fold the top into a second triangle. Fold the one triangle over the other to close. Place a pat of butter on each triangle and brown on a sheet pan in the oven for 15 minutes. You may also sauté the triangles until brown in a small frying pan.

4. To make the honey sauce, caramelize the honey in a saucepan. Add the orange juice and the saffron stigmas. Reduce the sauce over high heat for 2 minutes. Swirl the sauce over the bottom of the plate. Stand the triangles of feuilles de brick so that they support one another in the middle of the plate and serve.

Fruitcake with Candied

3 cups/500 g confectioners' sugar
2¾ cups/700 g butter
5⅔ cups/725 g flour
5 eggs
2 tsp/20 g baking powder
2 tsp/20 g cinnamon
2 cups/500 ml custard (see
  basic recipe)
3½ oz/100 g kumquats

1¼ cups/300 ml sugar syrup (see
  basic recipe)
6½ tbsp/100 ml dark rum
⅔ cup/100 g candied citron
¾ oz/20 g hazelnuts

For the garnish:
4 fresh kumquats
8 candied cherries

Serves   4
Preparation time: 30 minutes
Cooking time: 1 hour 20 minutes
Resting time: 1 hour
Difficulty: ★

Although basic recipes for fruitcake are all more or less the same, the variations on fruitcakes are endless. Raisins, almonds, oranges, melon, angelica, ginger—any fruit that may be candied   will work in this recipe. Here, the choice of fruit is based on color: Our chef brings together the pale green of the citron, the orange of the kumquats and the bright red of the cherries in the conception of this dessert.

As to the other flavors in the fruitcake, we recommend using a high-quality sweet butter to give the cake the best possible taste. Dark rum enhances the butter and fruit flavors, though it can be replaced by orange liqueur or vanilla. This fruitcake will keep well for several weeks wrapped up in the refrigerator.

Measure all ingredients carefully for this dessert, particularly the flour and sugar, for too much of either will make the candied fruit sink to the bottom of the cake. One way to insure the candied fruit is distributed evenly is to coat the it in a little of the flour before adding it to the batter.

We have garnished the cake with brightly colored pieces of fresh and candied fruit along with orange-flavored custard. A kumquat custard also makes a fine accompaniment.

1. To prepare the cake batter, beat together the confectioners' sugar and softened butter. Add the eggs. Stir in the flour, baking powder and cinnamon. Let the batter rest for 1 hour.

2. Soak the candied citron in the rum overnight. Drain and reserve the rum. To candy the kumquats, cook them over high heat in the sugar syrup for 20 minutes. Drain and reserve the sugar syrup. Chop all of the candied fruits and hazelnuts and add them to the cake batter.

Citron and Kumquats

3. Bake the fruitcake in a buttered and floured loaf pan for 1 hour at 350 °F/180 °C. The fruitcake is done when a knife stuck into the center comes out clean.

4. Reheat the reserved rum and kumquat syrup and grush the top of the fruitcake with the hot syrup mixture. Allow the cake to cool for 10 minutes in the loaf pan, then unmold and allow to cool. Cut the cake into slices. Place the slices on the plate with the orange custard and the bits of candied fruit for garnish.

Cassolette Claudia with

1 cantaloupe
1 mango
½ pineapple
1 banana
4 tbsp/50 g brown sugar

For the sauce:
juice of 1 orange
½ tsp cardamom
½ tsp allspice

Serves 4
Preparation time: 15 minutes
Cooking time: 10 minutes
Difficulty: ★

In the Caribbean, individual servings of caramelized fruit are often served at the end of a light meal. Cassolette is the French word for an individual-sized frying pan with lid used both to cook and serve sweet or savory items. We suggest using copper cassolette pans for this dessert, though the fruit may also be presented piping hot on a plate surrounded by small scoops of ice cream.

This dessert should be prepared just before serving to avoid overcooking: Allowing the fruit to remain in its cooking juice will cause it to soften further and lose much of its shape. Place the various kinds of fruit into the hot caramel one at a time, beginning with the cantaloupe and mango, which require longer

to cook. The bananas and pineapple should be added last. Once the fruit is nearly cooked through and thoroughly coated with the caramel, deglaze the cassolette with orange or other citrus juice. Papaya or passion fruit juice may also work well here.

Feel free to improvise on this dessert using whatever fruit you have at hand or whatever is in season and readily available. You may also substitute the spices suggested here by our chef with vanilla, coriander or cloves.

As a grand finale, you may wish to flambée the cassolettes at the table: In a small saucepan, warm a little aged rum or Triple Sec. Ignite the alcohol in the pan and quickly pour the flaming liquid over the cassolettes.

1. Cut the mango, cantaloupe and pineapple into thick triangles. Slice the banana diagonally.

2. In a large frying pan, cook the brown sugar to a light caramel. Add the cantaloupe and the mango and cook for 2 minutes, then add the banana and pineapple, which require less cooking time.

Caramelized Caribbean Fruit

3. When the fruits are almost done, deglaze the pan with the orange juice and add the spices. Allow the juice to reduce with the caramel until thickened.

4. Place 2 pieces of each fruit into each individual cassolette pan. Arrange the fruit pieces on top of one another to form a small dome. Drizzle the fruit with the orange-caramel sauce and serve hot.

Caramelized

2 cups/500 ml heavy cream
2 cups/500 ml milk
12 egg yolks
1 cup/250 g sugar
4 cinnamon sticks
zest and juice of 2 oranges
1⅓ cup/250 g granulated brown sugar

For the garnish:
1 orange
1 cup/250 ml water
1 cup/250 ml sugar syrup (see
  basic recipe)

Serves	*4*
Preparation time:	*15 minutes*
Cooking time:	*2 hours*
Chilling time:	*1 hour 30 minutes*
Difficulty:	*★*

Cinnamon is actually the bark of a tropical tree. When the bark is dried, it curls up into reddish-brown sticks and gives off a strong, distinctive aroma. In large quantities, cinnamon adds a hot, spicy flavor. This recipe calls for cinnamon sticks not rather than cinnamon: Ground cinnamon would fall to the bottom of the flan and leave a black residue in the ramekins.

Infuse the cinnamon and orange zest in the milk and cream a day in advance so the orange zest has time to release its flavor and the liquid absorbs the full flavors of cinnamon and orange. It is very important to beat the egg yolks and sugar to ribbon consistency before adding the hot milk and cream. The smooth, creamy texture of the flans depends on this, as it keeps the sugar from burning the egg yolks and forming lumps.

Fill the ramkeins carefully to the top with the flan custard, avoiding spills and overflows, and bake in a warm oven. Make sure the water in the pan does not come to a boil: It should just simmer until the flans are set.

To candy the orange slices, blanch them in water to remove all bitter taste, then drain. Bring the slices to a boil in the sugar syrup, remove from the heat and allow to cool. You may vary this recipe by substituting pomelos or mandarin oranges for the oranges used here, or by flavoring with vanilla, anise or ginger instead of the cinnamon.

Once the flans have cooled, sprinkle them lightly with the granulated brown sugar and caramelize the tops with a hot iron or under the broiler. Decorate with a slice of candied orange.

1. In a saucepan, bring the milk cream and orange juice to a boil, and add the cinnamon sticks and zest. Cover and allow to infuse for 15 minutes.

2. Beat the egg yolks with the sugar to ribbon consistency. Bring the milk and cream back to a boil and add to the egg mixture, whisking continually.

Orange Flan

3. Pass the flan custard through a fine strainer to remove the cinnamon and orange zest and place in refrigerator. While the custard is chilling, candy the orange slices.

4. Fill the ramekins and place them in the oven in a pan filled half filled with water for 2 hours or until the flans are set. Allow to cool, then sprinkle with the brown sugar and caramelize under the broiler. Serve immediately.

Banana Charlotte

For the charlotte bread:
12 slices of white bread
½ cup plus 2 tbsp/150 g butter
4 vanilla beans

For the banana filling:
1 lb bananas
3½ tbsp/50 g butter
6 tbsp/75 g brown sugar
a pinch of allspice

For the coffee cream:
1 cup/250 ml milk
½ cup/125 ml expresso or very
    strong coffee
4 egg yolks
5 tbsp/75 g sugar

Serves   4
Preparation time: 1 hour
Cooking time: 25 minutes
Difficulty: ★ ★

This dessert was named for Queen Charlotte of England in the eighteenth century. A relatively easy dessert to assemble, the classic charlotte requires no baking. It is made by lining a mold with ladyfingers soaked in liqueur or fruit juice then filling the lined mold with a vanilla or fruit-flavored mousse and served chilled or at room temperature.

Since it was first introduced, the charlotte has undergone countless transformations and is served in one form or another around the world. Our chef has varied the classic charlotte recipe by replacing the ladyfingers with simple white bread. Sponge cake may also be used to surround the banana filling used here.

The bread used to line the charlotte mold must be brushed with melted butter so that it remains soft when baked. Pay close attention when cooking the charlotte so that the bread browns but does not turn to toast.

The charlotte presented here may also be made with apples, pear or jackfruit filling. Instead of allspice, you may use vanilla, nutmeg or cloves to flavor the filling.

When plating the dessert, coat the plate with the coffee cream. Pipe small drops of heavy cream onto the coffee cream. Draw out thin swirls of the heavy cream using the tip of a small knife or a toothpick for a star decor in the coffee cream.

1. Peel the bananas and cut them into small cubes. Place the diced bananas in a saucepan with the butter, brown sugar and allspice, and simmer until the bananas have cooked down into a thick compote.

2. Remove the crust from the bread. Cut 4 of the slices into 4 strips, then cut each of the strips in half. From the remaining slices, cut 4 larger circles and 4 smaller circles corresponding to the size of the tops and the bottoms of the charlottes, Generously coat the slices and circles with melted butter.

with Coffee Coulis

3. Butter and sugar the charlotte molds, and place the large buttered circle of bread at the bottom of the mold. Line the sides of the mold with the strips of bread. Fill the charlotte with the banana compote and close it with the smaller circle of bread.

4. To prepare the coffee cream, bring the expresso and milk to a boil in a saucepan. Whisk the eggs with the sugar. Pour the hot liquid into the egg mixture, whisking continually. Return the sauce to the pan and place over low heat, stirring constantly. Bake the charlottes for 20 minutes at 375 °F/190 °C. Coat the bottom of the plate with the coffee sauce, place the hot charlotte in the center, and serve.

Lime

juice of 1 lime
⅔ cup/150 ml sugar syrup (see basic recipe)
15-20 ladyfingers

For the lime cream:
juice of 3 limes
6½ tbsp/100 g sugar
6 gelatin sheets
3 cups/750 ml whipping cream

Serves	*4*
Preparation time:	*1 hour*
Chilling time:	*1 hour*
Difficulty:	★ ★

Although it is now considered a classic French dessert, the first charlotte was created in England at the end of the 18th century and named for the wife of King George III. In the traditional charlotte, a slightly tapered round mold is lined with buttered slices of white bread, ladyfingers or sponge cake soaked in sugar syrup and fruit juice, then filled with a fruit compote flavored with cinnamon and lemon.

Here, we have a chilled charlotte variation. The lime, that small, round, juicy green cousin to the lemon, lends a tart fresh flavor to the charlotte. Six sheets of gelatin hold the lime cream together. Our chef recommends using more gelatin for charlottes made with acidic fruits than for those made with sweeter fruits like apples or pears to keep the acid from breaking down

the whipped cream. Otherwise, this basic recipe for a chilled charlotte can be used for all types of fruit. It is particularly good made with berries. Vary the sauces you make to accompany this dessert according to the fruit you choose to use.

As a garnish to this dessert, we suggest candied lime zests and a light lime jelly. For the candied zest, boil the lime peel in two cups of sugar syrup until it becomes translucent. To make a lime jelly to coat the bottom of the plate, warm the juice of two limes. Soften a sheet of gelatin and add it to the warm juice, stirring to make sure the gelatin is completely dissolved. Pour a small amount of the warm lime jelly into the bottom of the plate, and place in the refrigerator until set. Put the charlotte in the center of the plate and decorate with the candied lime zest.

1. Heat the sugar syrup with the juice of 1 lime. Soak the ladyfingers in the lime syrup until soft but not soggy.

2. Whisk the juice of the 3 limes with the sugar. Soften the gelatin and melt it by placing it in the microwave for several seconds. Add the melted gelatin to the lime juice and sugar. In a separate bowl, whip the cream until it forms stiff peaks. Fold the whipped cream into the lime juice and gelatin mixture.

Charlotte

3. Butter the charlotte molds and coat them with a thin layer of sugar. Line the bottom and the sides of the molds with the soaked ladyfingers.

4. Fill the charlotte mold with the lime cream then cover the top with ladyfingers. Refrigerate 1 hour, unmold and serve chilled on a plate garnished with lime jelly and candied limes.

Plantain-Peanut

1½ cups/400 g puff pastry
    (see basic recipe)
1 egg yolk

For the banana filling:
3 plantains
1 cup (scant)/150 g peanuts
⅓ cup/80 g butter
2 tbsp/30 g sugar

Serves   4
Preparation time: 35 minutes
Cooking time: 35 minutes
Difficulty: ★ ★

Plantains, which resemble bananas, have a green skin and a light pink flesh that is firmer than that of a yellow banana. Plantains are generally larger and longer than bananas and contain more starch and less sugar. We have chosen to use plantains in the turnover recipe given here because of their high starch and low juice content. Apples, pears or other fruits with a low juice content may also be used in turnovers. Avoid using juicy fruits such as berries as they make the turnover filling too liquid and too much like a puree rather than a compote.

Once the plantains are peeled and diced, roast them with the peanuts, butter and the sugar over high heat until they are lightly caramelized. Chill the filling completely.

To form the turnovers, cut the puff pastry into circles. Place a spoonful of filling in the center of each circle. Using an egg yolk, egg wash the edges of the circle. Close each circle in half around the filling, making sure to seal the puff pastry completely. Egg wash the tops of the turnovers then score them with the back of a paring knife in the desired pattern. Bake the turnovers in a hot oven.

This turnover is best served warm straight from the oven, but it is also delicious when reheated. A serving suggestion: Warm the turnovers in the oven the next morning for a particularly special breakfast treat.

1. Roll out the puff pastry dough to the desired thickness. Chill before cutting into circles for the turnovers.

2. Pan-roast the plantains and peanuts with the butter and sugar over high heat for 10 minutes. Remove from the pan and allow to cool.

Turnover

3. Fill the turnovers with the plantain-peanut mixture. Wash the edges of the puff pastry circle with egg and fold the circle in half to close the turnover. Crimp the sides with the back of a knife to seal both edges of the puff pastry together. Glaze the top of the turnover with egg.

4. Using the back of a paring knife, decoratively score the pastry to enable the steam to escape, Bake the turnover at 375 °F/190 °C for 25 minutes or until golden brown.

Marbled Chocolate Fish

5¼ oz/150 g white chocolate
5¼ oz/150 g dark chocolate
5¼ oz/150 g litchis

For the ganache:
8¾ oz/250 g bittersweet chocolate
⅔ cup/150 ml whipping cream
¾ cup/200 ml litchi liqueur

For the jelly:
¾ cup/200 ml curaçao
1 gelatin sheet

Serves	4
Preparation time:	1 hour
Cooking time:	10 minutes
Chilling time:	15 minutes
Difficulty:	,★ ★ ★

To make the marbleized chocolate used in this dessert, choose high-quality white and dark chocolates which will temper easily and develop a brilliant sheen when cooled. To temper the chocolates, break them into small pieces so that they melt evenly and stir the mixture continually over low heat to eliminate lumps and scorching.

Chef's hint: Test the temperature of the chocolate by touching a spoonful of chocolate to your lips. If the temperature is right, you will feel neither heat nor cold.

Once the chocolates are tempered and are uniform in temperature, pour them onto a sheet of florist's plastic with a small ladle and swirl into a thin layer of chocolate with a palette.

Allow the chocolate to set before cutting into shapes. Any shape of cutter will do, but it should be made of metal so it can be warmed before cutting the chocolate.

The litchi liqueur used in the ganache brings out the flavor of the fresh litchis, but there are many other excellent flavor combination: You might want to try raspberries and chambord or oranges and Triple Sec.

The jelly used to garnish the plate is made by mixing hot curaçao with a softened sheet of gelatin. Pour the warm jelly onto the bottom of each plate then chill until set, then place the marbleized fish in the center of each plate.

1. Temper the white and dark chocolates separately by warming them to 85 °F/30 °C. Prepare the ganache filling by melting the bittersweet chocolate then stirring in the warmed whipping cream and liqueur.

2. Drible lines of white and dark chocolate onto the florist's plastic and cover with a second piece of plastic to insure the layer of chocolate remains thin. Use a rolling pin to spread the chocolates evenly between the plastic sheets. Prepare the curaçao jelly to be used to garnish the plates. Pour the jelly into the bottom of each plate and chill for at least 15 minutes.

with Litchi Ganache

3. Using a metal cutter, stamp out the marbleized chocolate into the desired shape. Warm the cutter each time you cut the chocolate by placing it for a few seconds on a hot baking sheet. Carefully peel and pit the litchis.

4. Pipe the ganache around the edge of a marbleized chocolate fish. Fill the center with the fresh litchis. Place another ganache-covered fish on top of the litchis, then repeat the filling procedure. Finish with a single marbleized chocolate fish.

"Enchanted Evening"

10¼ oz/300 g baked brioche (see
   basic recipe)
⅔ cup/150 ml milk
6½ tbsp/100 ml whipping cream
1 vanilla bean
3 eggs
5 tbsp/70 g sugar
14 oz /400 g pineapple

For the "Romantic Interlude" cocktail:
¼ cup/50 ml pineapple juice
¼ cup/50 ml strawberry juice
½ cup/100 ml champagne

Serves   4
Preparation time: 30 minutes
Cooking time: 35 minutes
Difficulty: ★ ★

The traditional *clafoutis*, made from crêpe batter and fresh, unpitted black cherries, stems from the Limousin region of France. The crêpe batter is poured over the cherries into the pan and baked in the oven. Many variations of the original clafoutis call for apricots, pears, mangos or kumquats.

For the pineapple clafoutis presented here, our chef has selected the elongated bottle pineapple, which is sweeter than the rounder versions more commonly found on the market. If you choose to use a round pineapple, be sure to taste it and adjust the sugar in the clafoutis batter accordingly.

The light, airy texture of this clafoutis comes from the yeast in the brioche used. While we have chosen to make individual servings of the clafoutis using small pans, it is possible to bake the clafoutis in a large round cake pan. A larger clafoutis will puff up more like a soufflé because of the yeast.

The oven temperature plays a large role in the success of this dessert. Correct baking temperature and adequate preheating are essential to allow the clafoutis to begin to bake the moment it is placed in the oven. Open the oven door only when absolutely necessary to avoid drastic changes in temperature which will keep the clafoutis from cooking evenly and may even cause it to fall.

The "Enchanted Evening" cocktail from which this dessert takes its name is presented as a garnish. Prepare the cocktail just before serving and swirl it around the bottom of the plate.

1. Cut the crust off of the brioche and cut the center into small pieces. Place the pieces in a bowl and reserve.

2. In a saucepan, bring the milk and cream to a boil with the vanilla bean. Allow the vanilla bean to infuse for several minutes then remove.

Pineapple Clafoutis

3. Pour the milk and cream over the small bits of brioche in the bowl and whisk together. Add the eggs 1 at a time then the sugar. Whisk until all ingredients are combined.

4. Dice the pineapple and stir it into the clafoutis mixture. Pour the clafoutis into the pans and bake for 30 minutes at 350 °F/180 °C. Unmold the clafoutis and serve with several drops of the "Enchanted Evening" cocktail as shown here, or coat the bottom of the plate with the cocktail as a sauce.

Karukera

1 cantaloupe
½ watermelon
3½ tbsp /50 ml Triple Sec

For the garnish: fresh mint leaves

Serves	*4*
Preparation time:	*10 minutes*
Freezingtime:	*1 hour*
Difficulty:	★

Simple and refreshing, the Karukera Dessert Cocktail is the perfect drink to have on hand for unexpected guests in the heat of the summer. Children will also clamor for this colorful treat which is quick to prepare and easy to store—and it provides a light alternative to milkshakes or smoothies. The distinctly separate bright colors which hold their lines in the glass will charm both guests and children alike.

Select fruits of various colors, as we have done here with the watermelon and cantaloupe. Although watermelon has relatively little nutritional value, it is both sweet and refreshing. Make sure to select a watermelon which feels heavy in hand and does not sound hollow when lightly tapped with your index finger.

Once its seeds have been removed, the melon may be used in this recipe, added to a fresh fruit salad, or even made into jam.

In order to achieve the two-tone look of this cocktail, our chef came up with the idea of using the fresh fruit purée in both liquid and frozen form. The juice of one of the fruits floats on top of a shaved ice granite of the other, keeping the colors separate and distinct. Granite, a kind of Italian ice which is shaved into bits as it freezes rather than being frozen in suspension like a sorbet, is simple to prepare. Place the fruit juices in the freezer and every fifteen minutes, scrape off the ice which form on the top. Carefully distribute the granite in the glasses then pour the fruit juices over them.

1. Remove the rind of the cantaloupe and scrape out the seeds. Using a melon baller, scoop out enough cantaloupe balls to decorate the cocktails. Purée the rest of the cantaloupe in a food processor until smooth, and add half the Triple Sec. Divide the juice obtained in half. Place one half in the refrigerator and half in a small, open container in the freezer.

2. Cut the watermelon into quarters and remove the rind and all seeds. From the center of the de-seeded watermelon, scoop out balls to be used later as a garnish; set aside. Purée the rest of the watermelon until smooth and add the remaining the Triple Sec. As in Step 1, place half of the resulting juice in the refrigerator and half in a small, open container in the freezer.

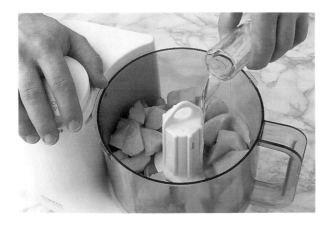

Dessert Cocktail

3. Once the granites have set, put them into the bottom of 4 stemmed glasses. Pour the chilled juices over the granites, alternating colors.

4. Garnish each glass with the melon balls and bits of finely chopped mint and serve immediately.

Creole

4 sheets phyllo dough
4 eggs
4 kumquats

For the ganache:
8¾ oz/250 g dark chocolate
⅔ cup/150 ml whipping cream
2 tbsp/30 ml corn syrup
⅔ cup/150 ml crème fraîche
4 candied kumquats

For the sabayon:
4 egg yolks
3½ tbsp/50 ml sugar syrup (see basic recipe)
6½ tbsp/100 ml expresso or strong coffee
2 tbsp whipping cream

Serves | 4
Preparation time: | 30 minutes
Cooking time: | 20 minutes
Difficulty: | ★

In the early 19th century, Grimond de la Reynière, the celebrated French gastronome, cited 543 uses for eggs. Since his time, this number has grown to almost a thousand—not to mention the symbolic use of eggs at Easter or Passover in western culture, or their use in celebrating the first month of a newborn's life in China. Cut the eggs with a sharp-pointed knife or even a pair of sharp scissors to give the dessert a sleek, professional look.

The *ganache* may be made in advance, but the sabayon must be prepared just before serving. The hot-and-cold element of surprise is of the essence in this dessert: The combination of the warm sabayon with the chilled *ganache* provides an intense and unusual taste experience.

Making the phyllo dough "plate" is perhaps the most time-consuming and difficult part of this recipe. The phyllo dough is best styled and baked at the last minute so that it holds its shape and light crispy texture. If you are pressed for time or find phyllo difficult to shape and handle, the eggs may be served in decorative egg cups. We recommend an aged rum or a small cup of hot expresso as accompaniment to this dessert.

1. Cut off the tops of each of the 4 eggs and even out the edges with a pair of scissors. Using your hands, separate the yolks from the whites and reserve the yolks for the sabayon. Wash the shells and allow them to dry, making sure not to crack or break them.

2. To make the sabayon, whisk the egg yolks, sugar syrup and expresso together in a saucepan over low heat for about 10 minutes until thick. Allow the sabayon to cool. Whip the cream to stiff peaks and fold it into the egg mixture.

Coffee Eggs

3. For the ganache, melt the chocolate in a double boiler. Add the whipping cream and corn syrup. Take the chocolate off of the heat and stir in the crème fraîche and candied kumquats.

4. Press ½ sheet of phyllo dough gently into an egg carton. Bake for 2 to 3 minutes in a hot oven until brown. Fill the egg shells half-full with the ganache-kumquat mixture, then pipe the sabayon over the ganache to the top of the egg shells and decorate with a slice of fresh kumquat.

Chocolate-Tipped

2¼ cups/200 g grated coconut
¾ cup plus 1 tbsp/200 g sugar
2 egg whites
2 oz/60 g dark chocolate

Serves	4
Preparation time:	10 minutes
Cooking time:	15 minutes
Drying time:	24 hours
Difficulty:	★

These petits fours, also called coconut rochers, are easy to prepare and make a stunning presentation at the end of a meal or as an accompaniment to tea or coffee.

Our chef recommends drying the coconut by leaving it in a warm sunny spot for 24 hours to eliminate any moisture which might cause the macaroons to fall while baking. If you do not have the time to sun-dry the coconut, place it in a slow oven for four to five minutes before assembling the macaroon batter.

The macaroons shown here were shaped using an aluminum pastry tip, but you may also use any other small shapes or molds

at hand: Circles, teardrops and pyramids will work as well. Small, bite-sized shapes make the best presentation.

Melt the chocolate over simmering water in a double boiler until it is warm but not hot and all bits of chocolate are melted. Dip the tip of each macaroon in the tempered chocolate. Shake off excess chocolate to prevent it from dripping down the sides of the macaroon. Set the macaroons upright to allow the chocolate to harden. These macaroons should be part of all petit four collections and can be served alongside other sweets such as fruit jellies and home-made chocolates or truffles.

1. Using a food processor or blender, chop the coconut until it resembles fine, coarse meal. Weigh the coconut and mix it with the same amount of sugar (by weight).

2. Stir the egg whites into the coconut-sugar mixture. The batter will be slightly moist and hold together when pressed gently.

Coconut Macaroons

3. Pack a small teaspoon of the macaroon mixture into the pastry tip. Blow into the hole of the pastry tip to unmold. Carefully place the macaroons on a non-stick baking sheet and bake for 15 minutes at 350 °F/180 °C.

4. Allow the macaroons to cool completely. Temper the dark chocolate in a double boiler. Dip the tip of each macaroon into the tempered chocolate and allow it to set before serving.

Tutti-Frutti

8¾ oz/250 g puff pastry (see
    basic recipe)
2 tbsp/30 g melted butter
½ mango
½ papaya
1 kiwi
½ guava
4 bunches red currants
½ passion fruit

4 Asian pears
½ grapefruit
¼ cantaloupe
6½ tbsp/100 g confectioners' sugar
⅔ cup/150 ml whipping cream
3 tbsp/45 g sugar
3½ tbsp/50 ml rum

Serves   4
Preparation time: 1 hour
Cooking time: 15 minutes
Difficulty: ★ ★ ★

In both ancient and modern times, a cornucopia brimming with flowers and fruit symbolizes wealth and abundance. Here, our chef has chosen to use this symbol in his dessert to emphasize the variety and abundance of tastes and colors that are found in tropical fruits.

The elements of the cornucopia dessert presented here are the same as those in a *mille-feuille* or napoleon: puff pastry, whipped cream and fresh fruit. Phyllo dough may also be used in place of the puff pastry.

When cutting the strips of puff pastry to make the cornucopias, measure the width of the strips carefully so that the rolls will be even around the cones. Use a large chef's knife to cut the puff pastry and avoid pulling on the pastry dough.

Select ripe fruits with a variety of colors and feel free to improvise on the choices given here. Segments the grapefruit and use a melon baller for the cantaloupe; cut the rest of the fruit into small thick quarters which will hold their shape.

The easiest way to assemble this dessert is to fill the cornucopia three quarters full with the whipped cream and top with a spoonful of fruit. Set the filled cornucopia on the plate before spooning the fruit around it. You may also coat the fruit with a light coulis made by blending one of the fruits with a little sugar syrup (see basic recipe). The fruit coulis will bring out the flavor of the fresh fruit, keep fruits like the mango and the Asian pears from turning brown, and add shine to the brilliant colors in the presentation.

1. Roll the puff pastry into a rectangle 23½ inches long, 3–4 inches wide and 1/16 in thick (60 cm x 10 cm x 1 mm). Cut the puff pastry into ¾ in/2 cm strips.

2. Butter the cornucopia molds and roll the puff pastry around them, starting at the pointed tip. Bake the cornucopias for 15 minutes at 350 °F/180 °C. Halfway through the baking time, sprinkle them with powdered sugar to give the pastry a sweet crisp, shiny crust. Carefully remove from the baking sheet and cool on a rack.

Cornucopia

3. Peel and slice the fruit, pick the red currants from their stems and stir the fruit together in a bowl. In a separate bowl, whip the cream until it forms soft peaks, then beat in the sugar and rum.

4. Fill each cornucopia with the rum cream and top with a spoonful of the fruit mixture. Set the cornucopia on a plate and place the rest of the fruit around it. Decorate the plate with a fruit coulis if desired and serve immediately.

Crispy Tropical Island

4 sheets of *feuilles de brick* (see
   glossary) or phyllo dough
1 egg white
2 tbsp/30 g butter

For the gum fruit compote:
3 gum fruit
½ cup plus 2 tbsp/150 g brown sugar
juice of 1 combava or lime
4 eggs

For the honey sauce:
5 tbsp/100 g honey
a pinch of nutmeg
a pinch of cinnamon
zest of 1 combava or lime

For the garnish:
4 mangosteens
2 oranges

Serves | 4
Preparation time: | 1 hour
Cooking time: | 25 minutes
Difficulty: | ★ ★

The gum, a tall tree whose sap is used to make chewing gum, bears a fruit which looks like a rough-skinned plum. The gum fruit has a light amber colored flesh and a grainy texture which make it a marvelous ingredient in fruit salads, sorbets or jams. Our chef has selected the gum fruit for the filling of this dessert, but apples, bread fruit or bananas may also be used. The slightly bitter taste of the gum fruit is paired with the sweet, smooth mangosteen and may be further complemented with a fruit coulis of your choice.

Crispy on the outside, light and tender on the inside, our pockets are mini-fruit soufflés enveloped in a shell of *feuille de brick* or phyllo dough. The filling recipe given here, which calls for egg whites, may also be used to make other kinds of fruit soufflés. Relatively low in fat and calories, this light dessert is recommended for the calorie-conscious who still want to enjoy a sweet treat every once in a while.

When arranging this dessert on the plate, carefully fan out the orange segments around the mangosteen. Place three pockets on the plate with generous pools of honey sauce between them as garnish. Sprinkle the plate with combava or lime zest for color.

1. Dice the gum fruit. In a saucepan, simmer the gum fruit and brown sugar over low heat for 10 minutes, adding the combava or lime juice at the end.

2. Separate the eggs. Stir the gum fruit compote into the egg yolks, and beat the egg whites to stiff peaks and fold them into the gum fruit mixture.

Pockets with Gum Fruit

3. Cut the feuilles de brick or phyllo dough into quarters. Place a small amount of the gum fruit filling in the center of each quarter and fold it into a rectangle. Seal the edges of the rectangle together by brushing them with egg white.

4. Melt the butter in a frying pan and sauté the pockets until brown. Drain and keep warm. For the honey sauce, pour off the excess butter from the pan and heat the honey. Add the combava zest and the spices. Arrange the crispy pockets on the plate with the mangosteen and orange. Decorate with generous amounts of honey sauce and serve immediately.

Sweet Lime Cream

2 cups/500 ml crème fraîche
zest of ½ combava or lime
2 gelatin sheets
¾ cup plus 3 tbsp/230 g
 granulated sugar

3 limes
1 sponge cake (see basic recipe)
3½ tbsp/50 ml sugar syrup (see
 basic recipe)
1 grapefruit

Serves   4
Preparation time: 20 minutes
Cooking time: 2 minutes
Refrigeration time: 25 minutes
Difficulty: ★

My kingdom for a lemon curd! Richard III could very well have cried this on the battlefield: Lemon curd became an extremely popular dessert in the 15th century, after a cook discovered by accident how to set lemon curd with eggs. Thereafter lemon curd was in high demand.

The recipe given here is for a lime cream rather than a lime curd. The eggs usually found in citrus curds are omitted and the cream is held together with gelatin. Our chef has chosen to use limes from the French Antilles along with the unusual combava in this dessert for an exotic twist on an old standard. This is a quick and simple dessert to prepare: It requires little equipment and uses ingredients which are easy to find on the market and store at home.

To simplify the preparation even further, store-bought ladyfingers may be used instead of the sponge cake which lines the bottom of the dessert. You may also use macaroons, sugar cookies or gingerbread for the biscuit at the bottom. Whichever biscuit you choose, be sure to soak it in sugar syrup and citrus juice before placing it in the bottom of the glasses.

The shape of the glasses used in servingthe dessert adds an elegant touch. Here we have used martini glasses but other stemmed glasses, ramekins or bowls will work just as well.

The three elements of this dessert—the sweet lime cream, the grapefruit segments and the soaked sponge cake—delight the palate with a variety of tastes and textures. Served chilled for a tart, refreshing finale to any meal.

1. For the creamy lime curd, bring the crème fraîche to a boil and add the combava or lime zest.

2. Soften the gelatin sheets in cold water. Add them to the crème fraîche along with the sugar and the juice of 2 limes. Place in refrigerator for 25 minutes.

with Grapefruit

3. Cut the sponge cake into rounds which will line the bottom of the glasses. Soak the rounds in sugar syrup and the juice of the third lime. Line the glasses with the sponge cake and spoon in the segments of the grapefruit.

4. Pour or spoon the chilled lime cream over the grapefruit segments and sponge cake. Sprinkle with lime zest and serve chilled.

Cinnamon-Mocha

6½ tbsp/100 ml strong coffee
  or expresso
2 cups/500 ml milk
2 cups/500 ml whipping cream
3 cinnamon sticks

1 cup/250 g sugar
6 egg yolks
¼ cup/60 g granulated brown sugar

Serves	*4*
Preparation time:	*15 minutes*
Cooking time:	*1 hour 45 minutes*
Refrigeration time:	*1 hour 30 mintues*
Difficulty:	★

The mocha and cinnamon flavors in this crème brûlée go well together without overpowering one another: Each remains distinct while complementing the other. Infuse the milk and the cream with the cinnamon and expresso long enough to give the crème brûlée a strong flavor of both. The coffee cream may also be infused with vanilla or lime zest instead of cinnamon.

The term "mocha" refers to any number of coffee-flavored desserts. It is, in fact, a type of coffee bean with a mild aroma and a smooth flavor. We suggest using a mocha expresso rather than a stronger, more bitter Italian expresso to flavor the crème brûlée featured here. Our chef strongly recommends using the finest coffee available such as Blue Mountain Jamaican, but you may use freeze-dried coffee instead of the mocha expresso.

Strain the milk and cream mixture to remove the cinnamon sticks and any residue, then whisk the hot mixture into the egg yolks and sugar. Pour the cream into small ramekins (or a baking dish), place in a larger pan two-thirds full with warm water, and poach in a 210°F/100°C oven until set. Cool completely and sprinkle with the granulated brown sugar.

To caramelize the sugar on top of the crème brûlée, use an iron made specifically for the task, or place the crème brûlées under the broiler for 2 to 3 minutes until the sugar caramelizes.

1. Brew an expresso or strong coffee. In a saucepan, bring the coffee, milk, cream and cinnamon to a boil and infuse for 10 to 15 minutes.

2. Separate the eggs. Whisk the yolks and sugar together, saving the whites for another recipe.

Crème Brûlée

3. Pour the cinnamon-mocha cream slowly over the eggs, while whisking constantly.

4. Divide the custard evenly among the ramekins. Poach in the oven in a water-filled pan at 210 °F/100 °C for 1 hour 30 minutes or until the custard is set, then chill for another 1 hour 30 minutes. Sprinkle generously with brown sugar and caramelize under the broiler for 2 or 3 minutes until the sugar begins bubbling.

Souffléd

For the crêpe batter:
1 cup/120 g all-purpose flour
3 eggs
2 tbsp/30 g sugar
1⅗ cups/400 ml milk
6½ tbsp/100 ml whipping cream
1 vanilla bean
2½ tsp/10 g melted butter
1 tbsp rum (optional)

For the coconut pastry cream:
1 coconut
1 cup/250 ml milk

3 egg yolks
8 tsp/40 g sugar
4 tbsp/30 g cornstarch

For the meringue:
5 egg whites
4 tsp/20 g sugar

For the garnish:
confectioners' sugar

Serves	4
Preparation time:	30 minutes
Cooking time:	35 minutes
Resting time:	2 hours
Difficulty:	★ ★
For the meringue:	

Crêpe batter must always be prepared ahead: It must rest at least 2 hours at room temperature or overnight in the refrigerator to devekop the elasticity of the gluten in the flour which are released when they are mixed with the liquid.

The recipe given here is for a classic crêpe batter and requires no special techniques. It is very important, however, that the batter be very smooth. If necessary, strain it through a sieve or chinois to eliminate lumps. If the crêpe batter seems too thick after the required rest time, thin it to the desired consistency with a small amount of water or beer.

We recommend making the crêpes thicker than usual so that they will not become brittle or tear when baked a second time with the soufflé. There are special pans with low sides and round, flat bottoms designed for making crêpes, or use a non-stick frying pan. Butter the pan lightly and pour a ladleful of batter into it, tilting the pan with a circular motion to distribute the batter. Pour off any excess batter. When the edges begin to turn brown, flip the crêpe and cook the other side. Slide the crêpe off of the pan onto a paper towel or a clean dish towel.

Serve the souffléd crêpes piping hot from the oven to prevent the crêpe from absorbing the cream and to keep the soufflé from falling before it makes its impressive appearance on the table. Our chef also recommends baking the souffléd crêpe directly in its serving dish to avoid damaging the crêpe. Once out of the oven, sprinkle the crêpes with confectioners' sugar and serve.

1. To prepare the crêpe batter, mix all of the ingredients in the order given, adding the milk slowly to the eggs, flour and sugar to avoid lumps. Scrape the seeds from the vanilla bean into the batter. Stir in the melted butter and rum last. Allow the batter to rest for 2 hours. Cook the crêpes in a buttered pan for about 3 minutes on each side.

2. To prepare the coconut pastry cream, bring the milk to a boil in a saucepan, mince the coconut and add it to the milk. Whisk the eggs with the sugar and cornstarch, stir a small amount of the hot milk mixture into the eggs to temper them, then add the eggs to the saucepan. Gently heat the cream for 10 minutes until thick.

Coconut Crêpes

3. Beat the egg whites to stiff peaks and gently fold them into the warm coconut cream in 2 batches.

4. Fill the crêpes with the soufflé mixture, smoothing the edges of the filled crêpe with a spatula to seal. Moisten the edges of the crêpe with water to prevent them from drying out and bake on a buttered sheet pan (or in a baking dish) at 425 °F/220 °C for 5 minutes. Serve immediately sprinkled with powdered sugar.

1 package phyllo dough
¼ cup /60 g melted butter
9 tbsp plus 1 tsp/140 g sugar
2 sweet potatoes
¾ cup plus 1 tbsp/200 g butter
¾ cup plus 1 tbsp/200 g brown sugar
¼ cup/50 g candied ginger, chopped

aluminum foil

For the honey sauce:
3 tbsp/70 g honey
juice of 1 lemon
1 oz/30 g fresh ginger root, grated

Serves	4
Preparation time:	35 minutes
Cooking time:	1 hour 20 minutes
Difficulty:	★ ★

Sweet

Sweet potatoes, which can have pink, purple or gray skins, were first imported to Africa from Asia by the Portuguese. With a higher sugar content than the common potato, the sweet potato can be used in sweet and savory recipes, and its flavor goes well with a wide variety of spices. You may also use bananas or apples in this crostada recipe.

Roast the sweet potatoes by wrapping them tightly in aluminum foil and baking them in a hot oven. Roasting the sweet potatoes conserves their flavor more than boiling. When the aluminum foil begins to swell, the potatoes are done. Test them with a knife, then mash them with a fork, allowing them to remain somewhat lumpy.

Cut each phyllo sheet into eight strips 2¼ in/6 cm wide, baste with melted butter and sprinkle with sugar. Lay the bands in a small blini pan with the buttered and sugared side down. Strengthen the bottom with an additional strip, folded in quarters.

Garnish the dessert with a simple honey sauce to bring out the flavor of the crostada. Coat the plate with the honey sauce , place the hot crostada in the center, garnish with julienned candied lemon and serve immediately.

1. Cut the phyllo sheets into bands. Baste each strip with butter and sprinkle with granulated sugar.

2. Cut the sweet potatoes in half. Dot them with butter, sprinkle with brown sugar and wrap tightly in aluminum foil. Bake for 1 hour at 400 °F/200 °C. Scoop out the potato flesh and mash with the candied ginger.

Potato Crostada

3. Cover the bottom of a blini pan with the strips of phyllo dough, buttered and sugared sides down. Place a folded strip of phyllo on the bottom to reinforce it. Fill the pan with the sweet potato mixture and close the strips of phyllo over top of the filling. Seal the strips with melted butter. Bake the crostadas for 20 minutes at 400 °F/200 °C.

4. While the crostadas are baking, prepare the honey sauce. Bring the honey to a boil. Add the lemon juice and grated ginger root. Garnish the bottom of the plate with the honey sauce, place the hot crostada in the center and serve.

Crispy Guava Purse with

4 medium-sized guavas
1 tbsp/30 g guava jelly
4 sheets phyllo dough
½ cup/125 g butter
3½ oz/100 g confectioners' sugar

2 vanilla beans, cut in half length-wise

For the frangipane:
3½ tbsp/50 g butter
6½ tbsp/100 g finely ground almonds
3½ tbsp/50 g sugar

For the chocolate sauce:
3½ oz/100 g dark chocolate
a pinch of ground cardamon

Serves	4
Preparation time:	35 minutes
Cooking time:	1 hour 20 minutes
Difficulty:	★ ★

A feast for the eye and palate, this chocolate-guava-phyllo combination will delight even the most demanding gourmet. The key to flavor is selecting only very ripe guavas and using a fine dark chocolate, preferably from the Caribbean. Cardamom enhances the subtle flavors of the other ingredients and adds an exotic touch.

The guavas used to fill the phyllo purses may be replaced by apples, bread fruit or apricots using the same techniques. Peel and seed the fruit, then fill it with jelly. Select a tart jelly to balance the sweet flavor of the ripe fruit for the filling.

While the phyllo dough provides a light and extra crispy crust for this dessert, regular puff pastry or *feuilles de brick* may also be used to form the fruit purses. Phyllo dough bakes very quickly, however, so take care not to overbake it.

The chocolate sauce is prepared by melting the chocolate in a double boiler and adding a pinch of cardamom. Dip the bottom of the baked guava purse into the melted chocolate, then set it in the center of the plate. Using the tip of a knife or a toothpick, draw small lines out of the chocolate surrounding the purse for decoration. The flavor associations in this dessert are what gives it its character. Feel free to improvise on the presentation and arrange the serving plate it in a different fashion.

1. Peel and seed the guavas and fill the centers of the fruit with the guava jelly. Baste 2 half-sheets of phyllo dough with softened butter and dust with confectioners' sugar. Place them, buttered and sugared sides down, in a criss-cross pattern in the bottom of the mold.

2. Prepare the frangipane by whisking together the softened butter, ground almonds and sugar. Fill the lined mold with the mixture.

Cardamom Flavored Chocolate

3. Place the filled guavas on top of the frangipane in the center of the mold. Carefully close the phyllo dough sheets over the top of the guava.

4. Tie up each guava purse with half of a vanilla bean cut lengthwise or fix with a toothpick. Bake for 15 minutes at 350 °F/180 °C, checking the phyllo regularly to make sure it does not turn too dark. Dip the bottom of the phyllo purse in the chocolate sauce and serve.

Barbados

¾ cup/200 g sweet dough (see
basic recipe)
4 cherimoyas (custard apples)
2 tbsp brown sugar
a pinch of cinnamon

For the crumble topping:
5 tbsp/75 g butter
4½ tbsp/50 g brown sugar
4½ tbsp/50 g ground almonds (see
    basic recipe)
¼ tsp/2 g cinnamon
2½ tsp/10 g flour

Serves	4
Preparation time:	30 minutes
Cooking time:	30 minutes
Refrigeration time:	30 minutes
Difficulty:	★ ★

Tea time in Barbados: This crumble, made with cherimoyas and cinnamon, is distinctly British with a tropical flair. The brown sugar used in the topping gives it a coffee-caramel flavor which complements the filling. Warm or cold, this dessert makes a wonderful afternoon snack served to friends.

The *cherimoya,* also known as custard apple, comes originally from Peru. About the size of an orange, it has a bumpy green skin which browns and blackens as the fruit ripens. The juicy white flesh, which has a sweet-and-sour taste with a hint of rose, is best eaten with a spoon when the fruit is very ripe. Cherimoyas are also excellent in fruit salads and sorbets.

All of the ingredients needed to make this recipe may be prepared in advance. The sweet dough may be kept in the refrigerator wrapped in plastic wrap. Store the cherimoya filling and the crumble separately in air-tight containers.

Roll out the sweet dough and score it with a fork or a roller. Cut the dough into rounds just larger than the tart circles to be lined, and allow the dough to rise up over the edge of the form to hold the crumble topping in place. The dough may be removed after baking with a sharp serrated knife.

The success of this dessert greatly depends on the quality of the crumble topping—a mixture of softened butter, sugar, ground almonds and cinnamon—which must be refrigerated until just before the crumble is baked. The topping should be lumpy and sandy-looking so that it will be crisp and crumbly when baked.

1. Roll out and score the sweet dough. Line four 4 in/10 cm tart rings with the dough and place on a nonstick baking sheet. Prebake the tart shells at 350 °F/180 °C for 15 minutes until lightly brown.

2. To prepare the cherimoya compote, peel the cherimoyas, remove the seeds and chop the flesh. Simmer the fruit with the cinnamon and brown sugar until soft and allow to cool completely.

Cherimoya Crumble

3. To make the crumble topping, stir together the softened butter, brown sugar ground almonds, cinnamon and flour. Chill for 30 minutes.

4. Fill the tart circles with the cherimoya compote. Rub the crumble topping between your fingers over the compote and bake approximately 12 minutes at 350 °F/180 °C until the crumble topping begins to brown. Serve warm or cold with a hot cup of tea.

Tropical

4 cups/1 liter milk
1 fresh coconut with milk
10 eggs
1 cup/250 g sugar

For the caramel:
6½ tbsp/100 g sugar
2 tbsp water

Serves	*4*
Preparation time:	*15 minutes*
Cooking time:	*1 hour 40 minutes*
Refrigeration time:	*30 minutes*
Difficulty:	★

Inside the tropical coconut is a sweet opaline liquid called the milk of the coconut. Whereas the white, flaky flesh of the coconut is often grated and used in desserts, our chef has created a treat calling for both grated coconut and the less frequently used coconut milk.

To flavor the custard, coconut milk, either fresh or canned, is infused in the regular milk. If you wish to use a fresh coconut, select one which is brown and ripe rather than young and green, for the milk of the mature coconut is thicker, sweeter and more flavorful than that of the unripe fruit.

You may season the coconut custard according to your own taste with vanilla, cinnamon or cane sugar and garnish it with drops of caramel. Chef's hint: To keep the caramel soft, add two

tablespoons of water after the sugar has cooked. Should you choose to make the dessert in ramekins or a baking dish, you may unmold it like a classic crème caramel before serving.

In this recipe, the coconut custard is presented in a half coconut shell. The baking directions, however, remain the same as for traditional baking dishes. Once the coconut shells are filled with the custard, they are baked in the oven in a pan of simmering water for 2 hours. Though it may require a bit more time and trouble, the use of the coconut shells turn an otherwise simple dessert into something exotic, and its flavor will delight true fans of caramel and coconut.

1. Scrape the flesh from the inside of the coconut and grate. Bring the milk, coconut milk and grated coconut to a boil. Set aside and allow to infuse for 15 minutes.

2. Whisk the eggs with the sugar. In a saucepan, prepare the caramel by cooking the sugar and water over high heat until the caramel turns a light brown.

Coconut Delight

3. Whisk the warm coconut mixture into the eggs and sugar mixture.

4. Pour the hot caramel into the bottom of the coconut shells or oven-proof baking dishes, then fill with custard and place in a pan of simmering water in the oven at 230 °F/110 °C. Bake for 1½–2 hours until the custard is set, then chill for 30 minutes in the refrigerator. Serve garnished with with a few drops of caramel.

For the fruit mousses:
½ cup plus 2 tbsp/150 g sugar
3½ tbsp/50 ml water
11 sheets gelatin
6 egg whites
4½ oz/125 g passion fruit
4½ oz/125 g coconut
4½ oz/125 g kiwi pulp
1 tbsp/15 ml dark rum
2 cups plus 6½ tbsp/600 ml
    whipping cream

For the tuile batter:
3½ oz/100 g chopped almonds
6½ tbsp/100 g sugar
3½ tbsp/25 g flour
2 egg whites
juice of 1 orange
2 tsp/10 g butter, melted

For the garnish:
3½ tbsp/25 g grated coconut

Serves	4
Preparation time:	1 hour 30 minutes
Cooking time:	10 minutes
Refrigeration time:	3 hours
Difficulty:	★ ★ ★

Fruit mousses became popular during the 1980's as a base in Bavarian creams and charlottes. These mousses were usually flavored with strong alcohols or liqueurs; our chef has instead chosen to flavor his three fruit mousses with only a small amount of dark rum to showcase the natural flavors of the fruits.

To save time, we recommend beating the egg whites and whipping the cream required for all three mousses then dividing the cream and meringue among the three fruit purées. A few drops of green food coloring may be added to the kiwi purée before incorporating the meringue and whipped cream to give it a brighter green color. If possible, prepare the mousses a day ahead so that they have time to set and completely absorb the fresh fruit flavors.

The fruit mousses are served with tuiles, small crisp cookies which are curled to look like the tiles found on roofs in the south of France. To shape the tuiles, have a piece of metal piping or a broomstick ready when they are removed from the oven. Wait one or two minutes until the tuiles begin to set then, working quickly, roll them around the tube to the proper shape.

1. For the Italian meringue, bring the sugar and water to a boil and cook the syrup to the soft ball stage (250 °F/120 °C). Soften the gelatin and add to the sugar syrup. Beat the egg whites to soft peaks and add the sugar syrup. Continue to beat until the meringue is cool, stiff and smooth.

2. Puree the passion fruit, coconut and kiwi separately, adding a teaspoon of rum to each. Whip the cream. To make the mousses: Fold equal amounts of the meringue and whipped cream into each of the fruit purées. Chill the mousses for at least three hours.

Delights

3. To make the tuiles, stir together the chopped almonds, sugar, and flour. Mix in the egg whites, orange juice and melted butter.

4. Using a spoon, spread the tuile batter onto a non-stick baking sheet and brown in the oven for 5 minutes at 300 °F/150 °C. Carefully remove the tuiles from the baking sheet, shape them or leave them flat, and arrange them on a silver serving tray. Pipe the fruit mousses into three small goblets and serve garnished with small amounts of each of the fruits and the grated coconut.

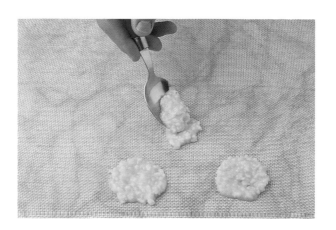

Citrus Dome

2 limes
2 grapefruit
2 pomelos
8 oranges
1¼ cups/300 ml tequila
5 sheets gelatin

For the garnish: (optional)
4 kumquats
mint leaves
orange zest

Serves — *4*
Preparation time: — *25 minutes*
Refrigeration time: — *1 hour*
Difficulty: — ★ ★

The well-known margarita cocktail served as inspiration for our chef when he created this dessert. Tequila and citrus complement one another for a fresh, tangy flavor. All citrus fruits work well in this dessert so feel free to substitute fruits such as mandarin oranges or tangerines according to availability.

Peel and segment the fruits on a cutting board with a grooved edge to catch all of the juice. This juice will be added to the tequila and softened gelatin mixture along with the juice of four oranges to make the jelly. Place the fruit segments in a shaped dish or mold. Here we have used a stainless steel mold, but cups, glasses and mousse molds work just as well.

Chill the molds in the freezer before assembling the dessert and place them on a bed of ice during assembly to make the jelly set faster. Brush the molds with a thin layer of jelly then add the fruit. After the first layer of fruit, pour in a small amount of jelly, allow it to set then add more fruit and repeat the operation until the mold is full. Chill the filled molds in the refrigerator until the jelly is completely firm. To unmold the dome, dip it quickly into hot water.

Placet the dome in the center of a plate and drizzle the remaining juice around it. Garnish the plate with finely chopped mint for color and flavor: The slightly peppery taste of the mint will set off the tangy, tropical flavors in this dessert.

1. Peel the limes, grapefruit, pomelo and 4 of the oranges on a grooved cutting board to catch all of the juice. Reserve all collected juice.

2. Working over a bowl, segment the fruit and remove the pith. Combine the tequila, the juice of the 4 remaining oranges and all the juice collected while peeling and segmenting the fruit. Macerate the fruit segments in this liquid for five minutes.

in Tequila Jelly

3. In a small saucepan, warm half of the tequila and fruit juice mixture. Soften the gelatin sheets and dissolve them in the warm fruit juice. Place the mold in a bowl of ice and brush it with a thin layer of the geled mixture and allow it to set.

4. Place the citrus segments in the mold, alternating colors. Pour more geled fruit juice over the fruit and allow to set. Fill the rest of the mold with the fruit segments and the geled mixture and chill for 1 hour until completely set. Unmold the domes, place in the center of the plates and garnish with the remaining geled tequila-citrus mixture, sliced kumquats, chopped mint leaves and orange zest if desired.

Mango and Guava Duo

2 small mangos
7 cups/1750 ml sugar syrup (see
   basic recipe)
2 star anise

For the guava sorbet:
8¾ oz/250 g guavas
6½ tbsp/100 g sugar
6½ tbsp/100 ml water
juice of 1 lemon

For the champagne sauce:
¾ cup/200 ml champagne
1 egg white

For the garnish:
4 branches rosemary
1 egg white

Serves	*4*
Preparation time:	*1 hour*
Freezing time:	*30 minutes*
Difficulty:	★

Our Mango and Guava Duo offers an uncommon combination of flavors in a spectacular dessert. The guava in the sorbet softens the peppery flavor of the poached mango while the champagne transforms an otherwise simple fruit dessert into something festive.

Peel and slice the mango. Plunge the mango slices in the hot sugar syrup flavored with the star anise and poach to soften the flesh. Remove from the syrup and drain. Chill the mango slices well so that the sorbet placed between the slices does not melt when the dessert is assembled.

Using a food processor or blender, purée the guava with its seeds to a smooth pulp. Three fourths of this puree will be used

in the sorbet. Blend the rest with the champagne and an egg white to make the frothy emulsified champagne sauce.

To assemble the dessert, place a scoop of guava sorbet between two mango slices and garnish with a frosted sprig of rosemary. Frosted rosemary sprigs can be made by dipping the rosemary in egg white and superfine sugar and then drying the branches in the oven for an hour at 200 °F/90 °C.

Two excellent alternatives to the champagne sauce are a fresh fruit coulis or an emulsified white wine sauce made by following the directions given here for champagne sauce. The fruits called for in the dessert may also be replaced by peaches or apricots.

1. Peel the mangos and cut two thick slices from each side of the pit. Peel the guavas and blend them into a smooth puree.

2. Poach the mango slices and the star anise in the sugar syrup over the lowest heat possible. Once they are soft, drain the slices and chill. For the guava sorbet, bring the sugar, water and lemon juice to a boil. Blend this syrup into the guava purée.

in Champagne Sauce

3. Set aside ¼ of the guava puree for the champagne sauce. Turn the rest of the purée in an ice-cream maker until it forms a thick sorbet.

4. For the champagne sauce, beat together the remaining guava purée, champagne and egg white. Place one slice of mango in the bottom of a tart ring, spread with a layer of sorbet and finish with a second slice of mango. Remove the fruit and sorbet from the tart ring and place in the center of the plate. Pour the champagne sauce over the dessert and garnish with a frosted rosemary sprig.

Tropical

For the garnish:
¼ cup/60 g sugar
4 tsp water
1 cantaloupe
4 pinches cinnamon
2 tbsp/20 g chopped pistachios

For the white chocolate mousse:
7 oz/200 g white chocolate
3½ tbsp/50 g melted butter
3½ tbsp/50 ml milk
3½ tbsp/50 ml orange liqueur
3 sheets gelatin
8 egg whites
¾ cup/200 ml whipping cream

Serves	*4*
Preparation time:	*50 minutes*
Cooking time:	*10 minutes*
Refrigeration time:	*50 minutes*
Difficulty:	★

Using a dome-shaped white chocolate mousse, melon balls and bits of hardened caramel, our chef has designed this dessert to look like a solar eclipse. The intense flavor of the centerpiece will be sure to please fans of white chocolate. We have used orange liqueur to enhance the creamy taste and texture and hint of vanilla that characterize white chocolate.

White chocolate is, in fact, not chocolate at all. Made with cocoa butter and skim milk, it does not contain the cocoa beans which give chocolate its distinctive taste and color. White chocolate is much more delicate to work with than dark chocolate. It must not be overheated when melted or the cocoa butter will separate from the milk solids. Our chef recommends breaking the white chocolate into small pieces and stirring the it constantly until the it has completely melted, and becomes smooth and shiny.

When arranging this dessert on the plate, garnish the domes of white chocolate mousse with broken bits of caramel for a three dimensional look. Small triangles of cinnamon and green pistachios can be used to represent the last rays of sunlight that appear before a total eclipse.

1. For the garnish, bring the sugar and water to a boil over high heat and cook until the caramel turns a light brown. Pour the caramel onto a sheet of aluminum paper and set aside to cool.

2. For the mousse, melt the white chocolate in a double boiler, and stir in the melted butter and milk. Warm the orange liqueur, dissolve the gelatin sheets in the orange liqueur, then add it to the white chocolate mixture. Beat the egg whites to stiff peaks and fold them into the white chocolate mixture.

Eclipse

3. Whip the cream to soft peaks and fold it into the mousse. Spoon the mousse into the dome molds. Chill for 50 minutes.

4. Once the caramel is cold, break it into bits with a mortar or a rolling pin. Unmold the mousse domes and place them in the center of the plate surrounded by melon balls, and insert bits of caramel into the top. Garnish the plate with the cinnamon and chopped pistachios.

Chocolate Mousse

For the chocolate mousse:
8¾ oz/250 g dark chocolate
6 eggs, separated
¼ cup/60 g sugar
2 cups/500 ml whipping cream
5 tbsp/50 g confectioners' sugar
1 passion fruit
a pinch of cocoa powder (optional)

For the fruit fan:
1 passion fruit
2 mangos

Serves   4
Preparation time: 30 minutes
Cooking time: 2 minutes
Difficulty: ★ ★

The flavors brought together in this dessert—mango, passion fruit and chocolate—complement without overpowering each another. The sought-after balance of tastes and textures found here characterize an exceptional dessert.

Native to India, the mango is a round green or oval fruit with yellow, red or violet markings. The orange flesh of the mango is luscious and juicy, well worth the effort required to remove it from the large pit found in the center. Because of this pit, only two thirds of the mango can be sliced and used.

Mangos are best eaten when just ripe, barely soft to the touch. Select mangos which feel heavy for their size and whose skin is smooth and unblemished: Black spots indicate the fruit is overripe and will be stringy.

The passion fruit is the product of a parasitical ivy which grows on trees in tropical climates. When ripe, the passion fruit has a wrinkled skin. The soft pulp encasing large, black, edible seeds, has a tart, distinctive flavor used sparingly in this recipe.

To balance the fruit flavors, we recommend a high-quality dark chocolate, that is rich in cocoa, thus guaranteeing a more refined flavor. When arranging serving plate, fan out the mango slices just beneath two quenelles of chocolate mousse and sprinkle them with cocoa powder before serving.

1. Break the chocolate into small pieces and melt in a double boiler, then whisk in the egg yolks. Beat the egg whites to stiff peaks together with the suga, then fold into the chocolate mixture.

2. Whip the cream with the confectioners' sugar until firm. Cut the passion fruit in half and scrape out the center with a spoon, then forl the soft passion fruit pulp and the whipped cream into the chocolate mixture. Add a dash of cocoa powder if desired.

and Mango Fan

3. Peel the mango and cut the two lobes from the pit. Slice the halves thinly with a sharp knife, then fan out the slices on a plate.

4. Pipe the mousse onto the plate or use two spoons to form quenelles. Garnish with passion fruit pulp and serve immediately.

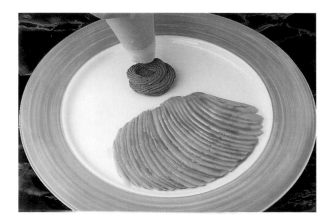

Mangosteen

1 package *feuille de brick* (see glossary)
1¼ cups/300 ml sugar syrup (see basic recipe)
¾ cup/100 g pistachios, finely chopped
¾ cup/100 g hazelnuts, finely chopped
3 lb 3 oz/1.5 kg mangosteens
1 tbsp confectioners' sugar

For the whipped cream filling:
6½ tbsp/100 ml whipping cream
4½ tbsp/50 g confectioners' sugar
1 vanilla bean or ½ tsp vanilla extract

Serves   4
Preparation time: 1 hour
Cooking time: 15 minutes
Chilling time: 30 minutes
Difficulty: ★ ★

The mangosteen is a succulently Asian fruit with a hard, thick skin and a mild white flesh. It can be served fresh, alone or in fruit salads—or it may be made into jam or ice cream. To keep the mangosteens from turning brown, peel and section them immediately before serving.

The pistachios and hazelnuts used to fill the feuille de brick layers in this recipe may also be replaced by peanuts, walnuts, cashews or almonds. Feuilles de brick can be bought at specialty gourmet stores or through mail order catalogs.

To make the feuille de brick triangles, cut each feuille de brick circle into eighths, then even out the rounded sides to form perfect triangles. Layer the triangles with the chopped nuts and bake on a non-stick sheet pan. Cover the triangles with parchment paper then weigh down with a heavy baking sheet to keep the feuilles de brick from shrinking and curling.

The mangosteen napoleons must be assembled at the last minute to keep the feuille de brick triangles from getting soggy. Peel and segment the mangosteens and place the sections around the whipped cream filling on the edges of the crispy feuille de brick triangles. Place one triangle on top of another with more mangosteen segments and cream. Finish with a third triangle decorated with confectioners' sugar. Garnish the plate with chopped pistachios and serve.

1. To cut the feuilles de brick, layer them on top of one another, then slice into 8 triangles and even out the edges.

2. Dip each triangle into the sugar syrup then place on a non-stick baking sheet.

Napoleon

3. Sprinkle each feuille de brick with chopped pistachios and hazelnuts then cover with a second triangle soaked in sugar syrup. Cover the triangles with parchment paper and weigh down with a baking sheet. Bake at 350 °F/180 °C for 15 minutes until light brown.

4. Whip the cream with the confectioners' sugar and the vanilla bean or extract. Place a spoonful of whipped cream in the center of a triangle then place the mangosteen segments around the cream. Repeat and finish with a third triangle. Decorate with confectioners' sugar and serve.

Crispy Chocolate Triangles

1¼ cups/300 g puff pastry (see
    basic recipe)
1 egg yolk
1 mango
2 tbsp sugar

For the chocolate pastry cream:
2 oz/60 g bittersweet chocolate
1¼ cups/330 ml milk
4 egg yolks
3½ tbsp/50 g sugar
⅓ cup/40 g flour

Serves	4
Preparation time:	1 hour
Cooking time:	20 minutes
Difficulty:	★

This dessert is a chocolate lover's delight: The rich flavor of bittersweet chocolate pleases the palate while the triangles of puff pastry add texture. Dark or bittersweet chocolate is delicate to work with and must be handled carefully. Variations in temperature change the consistency of the chocolate, and the proper texture will be lost if the chocolate is melted too quickly.

The scored decoration of the puff pastry has both aesthetic and practical value. Brushing the puff pastry with egg yolk and scoring it with the back of a knife not only make the turnover a decorative object in itself, it also allows the puff pastry to develop better while baking. We suggest using pastry made with butter rather than margarine. Although butter is harder to work with, the result will be lighter and more flavorful. Roll out

the dough and let it rest for 10 minutes to keep it from shrinking while baking, then cut it into triangles and bake. Cool the triangles before cutting them in half with a serrated knife.

Choose a firm, ripe mango which will not disintegrate when caramelized. Prepare the caramel, then cook the mangoes over high heat so that they take on the caramel color but retain their shape. As a garnish, the caramelized mango slices will complement the flavor of the puff pastry and add attractive color.

This dessert may also be made with a vanilla or coffee pastry cream and garnished with a fruit coulis (papaya and mango make good choices) or a basic chocolate sauce.

1. Roll out the puff pastry to ⅛ in/4 mm thickness. Cut the dough into 4 squares of 4 in/10 cm, then cut the squares diagonally to make 2 identical tirangles. Brush each of the triangles with egg yolk and score with the back of a knife. Bake at 375 °F/190 °C for 15 minutes.

2. Peel the mangos and cut each lobe into thin slices. Cook the sugar to a light caramel then add the mango slices. and allow them to caramelize for 2 to 3 minutes. Drain the slices and reserve the caramel liquid to garnish the plate.

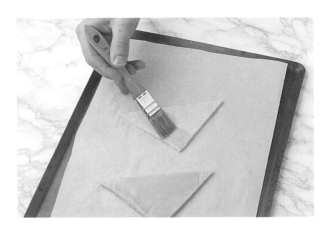

with Caramelized Mango

3. In a saucepan, melt the chocolate in the milk and bring to a boil. Whisk the eggs and sugar together in a bowl then add the flour. Pour the chocolate milk into the egg mixture, whisking constantly. Return the cream to the saucepan and cook for 2 to 3 minutes, whisking constantly.

4. Cut each puff pastry triangle in half. Place the bottom half of the triangle on the plate. Pipe small rounds of pastry cream onto the bottom layer. Cover with the top. Fan the caramelized mango out next to the turnover and garnish the plate with the reserved caramel sauce.

Anise and Cola

For the ice cream cone batter:
¼ cup/30 g buckwheat flour
4 tsp/10 g all-purpose flour
2 tsp/10 g sugar
2 egg whites
8 tsp/40 g melted butter
2 tsp crème fraîche

For the anise-cola mousse:
1 cola nut
¾ cup/200 ml anise syrup
¾ cup/200 ml whipping cream
4 egg whites

For the garnish:
4 tbsp/30 g pistachios, finely chopped

Serves	*4*
Preparation time:	*50 minutes*
Cooking time:	*15 minutes*
Resting time:	*1 hour*
Difficulty:	★ ★

Buckwheat was carried from Asia to Europe, where it has been cultivated since the end of the fourteenth century. Best known best for its use in pancakes, crêpes and blinis, buckwheat may also be cooked into porridge or used for stuffing. Although buckwheat is high in minerals such as vitamin B, the flour is low in gluten and therefore cannot be used to make bread. Its grain is black and yields a greyish flour. The black-flecked grey gives the shooting stars their distinctive color in this recipe.

The cola nut, native to Africa and South America, is a well-known stimulant, similar to coffee though not as strong. The cola nut donates its flavor to this recipe to balance out the strong flavor of anise in the mousse.

Feel free to improvise with the shape of the shooting stars. The batter may be spread into squares, circles or points as shown here using a metal spatula or a pastry bag. This batter may also be used to make garnishes for fruit mousse, sorbet or, as the name would indicate, ice cream. Whatever the use and shape, remove the shooting stars from the baking sheet the moment they come out of the oven. Because the batter is spread thin, the resulting cookies are very fragile once they cool.

Here we have given an otherwise simple combination a sophisticated presentation, resulting in a elegant dessert.

1. To make the ice cream cone batter, whisk together all ingredients in the order given. Let the batter rest for 1 hour before using

2. Using the tip of a metal spatula, spread the batter in a circular motion onto a non-stick baking sheet to obtain the shooting star motif. Scrape away any excess batter, and bake at 350 °F/180 °C for 10 to 15 minutes until light brown.

Nut Shooting Star

3. Cook the anise syrup to soft ball stage (250 °F/120 °C). Beat the egg whites into soft peaks, then add the anise syrup in a steady stream. Beat the meringue until cool. Whip the cream to soft peaks and fold it into the meringue. Season with grated cola nut and chill.

4. Place a spoonful of mousse on the plate. Set a shooting star on top of the mousse, then repeat. Garnish the plate with chopped pistachios and grated cola nut and serve immediately.

Kumquat Flan

For the flan:
2 cups/500 ml milk
10 kumquats, chopped
3 eggs
1 egg yolk
6½ tbsp/100 g sugar
4 tsp butter

For the jellied sauce:
juice of 1 orange
4½ tbsp/50 g brown sugar
3½ tbsp/50 ml orange liqueur
2 sheets gelatin
5 kumquats, sliced

For the garnish:
mint leaves

Serves	*4*
Preparation time:	*25 minutes*
Cooking time:	*25 minutes*
Refrigeration time:	*30 minutes*
Difficulty:	*★*

The word *flan* derives from the Gallic term *flado* used to describe flat objects. Originally, a flan was a sweet tart filled with a baked egg custard. Today, flan refers to a molded or upside-down steamed custard which can be flavored in a variety of ways. We have chosen the subtle flavor of the kumquat to season our flan, which goes well as a tea-time treat for friends or as a light dessert at the end of a family dinner.

Kumquats come from China though they are now grown all over Asia as well as in the warm regions of North America and Australia. They are eaten whole, tender skin and all. Because they resemble miniature oranges, kumquats are often used as a garnish for desserts. Its sweet, tart flavor makes the kumquat an ideal fruit for jam, marmalade or candied fruit

Only the freshest ingredients should be used to prepare the flan and the oven temperatures and cooking times given here must be respected. Place the ramekins with the custard in a pan of simmering water in a low oven. Check the flans often to avoid overcooking; the flans should be steamed until just set.

To make the pearls in the jelly on the plate, chill the plates garnished with the jelly sauce then pour small drops of liquid jelly sauce onto the set jelly. Decorate the flans with a small sprig of fresh mint and serve chilled.

1. To make the flan custard, bring the milk to a boil and steep the chopped kumquats in it. Whisk together the eggs, egg yolk, sugar and melted butter, then strain the hot milk and whisk it into the egg mixture.

2. Pour the custard into 4 small ramekins and place them in a pan of water. Steam the custard in the oven for 25 minutes at 275 °F/140 °C, then allow to cool.

with Pearled Jelly

3. Run a knife around the edges of the flans and unmold them directly onto the serving plate.

4. In a saucepan, bring the orange juice, sugar and sliced kumquats to a boil. Soften the gelatin sheets in cold water and add to the fruit syrup. ,Pour the sauce around the flan and refrigerate for 30 minutes.

Magic Flute

1 kiwi
1 pomegranate
½ pineapple
1 mango
1 cactus pear

For the "cigarette" batter:
8 oz/225 g confectioners' sugar
1½ cups/175 g flour
10 tbsp/150 g butter, melted
4 egg whites

For the whipped cream (see basic recipe):
2 cups/500 ml whipping cream
7 oz/200 g confectioners' sugar

Serves	*4*
Preparation time:	*30 minutes*
Cooking time:	*10 minutes*
Chilling time:	*15 minutes*
Resting time:	*24 hours*
Difficulty:	★ ★

The originality of this dessert comes from the arrangement of the filled "cigarette" on the plate—a faintly sweet, light, crispy cookie which goes just as well with breakfast fare as it does at the end of a good meal.

The cigarette batter is simple to make; the key to its success is allowing it to rest for 24 hours, then baking it on a non-stick sheet until it browns evenly. Before baking, make a test cookie with a small amount of batter: If the resulting cookie seems too fragile, thin the batter with melted butter and an egg white until the desired consistency is obtained. Shape the cigarettes in front of an open oven to keep the batter hot and malleable.

The cigarettes may be filled with the basic whipped cream recipe given here, or you may flavor the whipped cream with fruit, orange liqueur, litchi liqueur or rum to enhance the taste of the fruit.

This magical musical score makes a grand finale for an excellent meal and will be sure to set off a concerto of applause from one and all.

1. To make the cigarette batter, stir the sugar and flour into the melted butter, then add the egg whites and chill overnight.

2. On a non-stick baking sheet, spread the batter into a thin rectangle using a plastic scraper. Bake at 400 °F/200 °C for 10 minutes, then squickly roll the rectangle around the handle of a wooden spoon. Once the cokie has cooled, cut the cylinder into cigarettes using a serrated knife.

Tropical Symphony

3. Divide the whipped cream into 5 parts. Purée half of each of the fruits and fold the purées into the whipped cream to make 5 flavored creams. Pipe the creams into the cigarettes and chill for 15 minutes.

4. Dice the remaining fruit. Place the cigarettes on the plate and garnish with the diced fruit. Be sure to match the diced fruit to the flavored cream inside each cigarette.

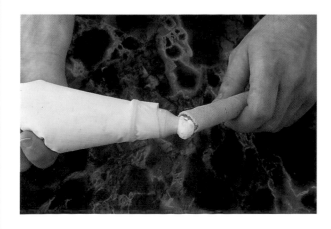

French Fried Mango

1 mango
1 pineapple
6½ tbsp/100 ml rum (optional)

For the fritter batter:
2 cups/250 g flour
½ tsp/5 g salt
1 cup/250 ml beer
3½ tbsp/50 ml oil
6½ tbsp/100 ml milk
3 egg whites

For the saffron sauce:
4 egg yolks
6½ tbsp/100 ml sugar syrup (see
   basic recipe)
a pinch of saffron
juice of 1 orange
8 tsp/40 g butter, melted
6½ tbsp/100 ml whipping cream

Serves | 4
Preparation time: | 30 minutes
Cooking time: | 18 minutes
Resting time: | 1 hour
Difficulty: | ★ ★

Have you ever thought of making french fries with something other than potatoes? Our chef had fun creating this french fried dessert made with pineapple and mango.

Select a ripe, sweet pineapple and a large firm mango, then cut fruits in the shape of french fries. To add flavor, macerate the fruit slices in rum and drain well before dipping them in the fritter batter and frying. The yeast and the beaten egg whites keep the batter light and crispy when fried. A helpful tip: Allow the batter to rest before coating the fruit use in order to give the yeast in the beer time to react and develop. This produces a wonderful fritter batter which will not absorb too much oil.

If you do not have a candy thermometer to test the temperature of the oil, you may check by frying a small spoonful of batter. If the it sizzles and browns quickly, the oil is hot enough for the fritters. After you have finished frying the fritters, allow the oil to cool, then strain it. The oil may then be used two or three more times for frying sweet ingredients.

The suggestions for garnishing and serving this dessert are in keeping with the french fry motif. The saffron sauce serves as a bright, exotic mayonnaise for dipping: Whereas Americans dip their fries in ketchup, Europeans usually prefer mayonnaise. Enjoy dipping the fruit fries in this spicy-sweet sauce and feel free to use your fingers! Serve the fries in cones made out of mangrove, palm or other large leaves to resemble the cones of fries served on street corners in Northern Europe.

1. To prepare the fritter batter, whisk together the flour, salt, eggs, beer, oil and milk. Beat the egg whites to stiff peaks, then fold them into the batter and allow to rest 1 hour.

2. Slice the pineapple and the mango into the shape of french fries and drain well.

and Pineapple

3. Dip the fries in the fritter batter and drop into the hot oil (340 °F/170 °C). Remove from the oil with a perforated ladle and drain well on paper towels.

4. To make the saffron sauce, whisk the egg yolks with the sugar syrup, saffron and orange juice in a saucepan over low heat. Stir in the melted butter and cool. Whip the cream to soft peaks and fold into the sauce. Serve the sauce with the french fried fruits.

Spiced Crisps, Fresh

For the spiced crisps:
5 tbsp/75 g butter, softened
5 tbsp/75 g sugar
3 egg whites
¾ cup/75 g flour, sifted
1¾ oz sesame seeds
a pinch of nutmeg
1 tsp/10 g red turmeric

2¾ oz/80 g *fromage blanc*
8¾ oz/250 g strawberries
1 clementine
2 kiwis
20 gooseberries

Serves	4
Preparation time:	35 minutes
Cooking time:	15 minutes
Difficulty:	★ ★

This lightly-spiced dessert brings together the creamy texture of *fromage blanc* and the crispness of thin spice cookies. The strawberries and other fruits add bright color and tart flavor to this refreshing taste treat.

If possible, select a full-fat fromage blanc or a thick, slightly sour yogurt which is high in acidophilus. A stronger-flavored fromage blanc such as this will bring out the natural flavors of the fruits. The fruits used in this recipe may be altered according to market availability. The strawberries, for example, may be replaced by raspberries, or by raisins plumped in hot water and alcohol, if strawberries are not in season.

Go lightly with the tumeric when seasoning the crisps so that the flavor of the spice does not overpower the fromage blanc. When preparing the spiced crisps, chill the non-stick baking sheet on which the batter will be spread in order to keep the butter in the batter from getting too soft. Our chef has made wavy, flame-shaped crisps by standing the crisps along the sides of a loaf pan while the crisps still hot, but this step is not required: You may allow the crisps to cool flat as well.

1. In a bowl, mix together the softened butter with the sugar. Gently fold in the egg whites, then stir in the flour, sesame seeds and nutmeg.

2. Spread the batter in the shape of flames onto a non-stick baking sheet and bake at 325 °F/160 °C for 15 minutes or until the crisps are browned evenly.

Fruit and Fromage Blanc

3. Cut each gooseberry in half, slice the kiwis and segment the clementines, removing all pith but retaining the pulp . Slice large strawberries in half but keep the smaller ones whole.

4. Spread the fromage blanc over the bottom of a shallow soup dish with a spoon. Distribute the prepared fruit over the fromage blanc, alternating colors and fruits. Delicately arrange the crisps around the fruit and serve immediately.

Caramelized Fruit with

2 apricots
2 peaches
2 plums
1 bunch of grapes

For the garnish:
4 mint leaves

For the four-pepper sauce:
a pinch of 4 peppercorn mix
3½ tbsp/50 g unrefined sugar
3½ tbsp/50 g butter
6½ tbsp/100 ml orange liqueur
juice of 1 orange
1 tbsp cornstarch

Serves	4
Preparation time:	20 minutes
Cooking time:	10 minutes
Difficulty:	★

The pepper plant is a climbing plant which originating in India. The pungent pepper blossoms develop into small green peppercorns which ripen to red or brown, and then become black when dry. Dry black peppercorns are most commonly used in Western cooking, but the others are also available on the market: green, white and red peppercorns, which you may even find freeze-dried. The heat and spice of the peppercorns' flavor comes from the essential oils they contain. Although rich in minerals, the oil becomes an irritant in strong doses and should therefore be used only paringly in recipes.

Other firm-fleshed fruits such as apples or papayas may be substituted for the fruits specified in this recipe. Cointreau, an orange-flavored liqueur, is only one of the possibilities which may be used to flavor the sauce.

Our chef has developed a light, peppery caramel which cooks the fruit quickly, coating it without allowing it to overheat and turn soft. To insure that the fruits remain firm, use a sauté pan which is large enough to hold all the fruit in one layer. Add the firmer-fleshed fruits to the caramel first, then the softer ones, so that they will emerge evenly cooked.

Drain the caramelized fruit in a colander to collect the juice. Reduce the juice by half, then bind the sauce with cornstarch diluted in a little water. We suggest serving this dessert with ice cream or a moist slice of pound cake.

1. Peel the peaches, and cut all of the fruit except for the grapes into large cubes.

2. Blanch the grapes in boiling water, peel and set aside.

Four-Pepper Sauce

3. To make the caramel sauce, cook the unrefined sugar with the butter and peppercorns until a light caramel forms. Stir in the orange liqueur and orange juice.

4. Add the fruits to the pepper sauce in the order listed in the list of ingredients and cook for 2 to 3 minutes over medium heat. Drain the fruit, collect the juices, then reduce and bind it with the cornstarch. Serve the fruit on a plate garnished with the pepper sauce and mint leaves and accompanied by ice cream or pound cake, if desired.

Spice-Route Poached Guava

6 guavas
4 slices gingerbread (see
  basic recipe)
3½ tbsp/50 ml white rum

For the wine sauce:
1 quart/1 liter red wine
6½ tbsp/100 g sugar
1 cinnamon stick
10 Jamaican peppercorns
3 star anise
1 pinch nutmeg
1 clove

For the honey ice cream:
9 egg yolks
¾ cup/200 ml honey
2 cups plus 6½ tbsp/600 ml milk
1 star anise
2 tsp orange-flower water

Serves	*4*
Preparation time:	*1 hour*
Cooking time:	*1 hour 10 minutes*
Freezing time:	*30 minutes*
Difficulty:	★

Native to Central America and the Antilles, guavas are small pear or apple-shaped fruits with a thin, yellowish skin that develops small black spots when ripe. The guava's refreshing, flavorful flesh can be orangish-pink, white or yellow; its center is soft with large black seeds.

For best results, select ripe guavas and a tannic red wine to poach them in. The star anise and Jamaican peppercorn used in the poaching liquid and sauce bring out the light flavor of the guavas, which are them served with honey ice cream to balance the spice in the sauce. The ice cream not only refreshes but also adds an interesting new texture to the ensemble.

Once the guavas have been poached in the wine and spices, reduce two cups of the poaching liquid to produce the shiny, maroon-colored sauce. Dip the poached guavas in the reduced sauce to coat them well and keep them from drying out. Slice two of the guavas to decorate the plates and place one whole guava on each of four plates with the remaining sauce.

Scoop a *quenelle* of the honey ice cream (vanilla or orange ice cream may also be used) onto the gingerbread round and garnish with a star anise.

1. Simmer the red wine for 45 minutes in a large saucepan together with the sugar and spices.

2. Peel the guavas and poach them in the reduced wine sauce for 15 minutes.

with Honey Ice Cream

3. For the honey ice cream, whisk together the yolks and honey. Bring the milk, star anise and orange-flower water to a boil, and allow to infuse for several minutes. Whisk the infused milk into the egg and honey mixture, then return the custard to the saucepan and poach for 10 minutes over low heat until thick. Chill completely, turn the custard in an ice cream machine, and set in the freezer for 30 minutes.

4. Place a whole guava at the top of the plate. Slice half of a guava and fan it out onto the plate. Cut a circle out of the gingerbread, brush it with rum and place a *quenelle* of honey ice cream on top. Garnish the plate with the spiced red wine sauce and serve.

Cluster of Grapes Fruit Salad

½ watermelon
6 kiwis
1 cantaloupe
¾ cup/200 ml whipping cream
2 tbsp/30 g sugar

1 cup/250 ml crème de menthe
2 sheets gelatin

For the garnish:
4 mint sprigs

Serves	4
Preparation time:	20 minutes
Cooking time:	2 minutes
Difficulty:	★

Here we give you the perfect remedy to the summer heat: What could be more refreshing than fresh fruit served with icy mint sauce?

Select the ripest, firmest fruits available to scoop into balls. Here we have chosen watermelon, kiwi and cantaloupe for the colors, but you may also use papayas, mangos, honeydew, or any other fruit in season.

In assembling this dessert, it is important to begin shaping the cluster of fruit at the tip and and move toward the base.

Once the overall shape is determined, pile the balls of fruit on top of each other, alternating colors.

The fresh fruit cluster is served with a lightly whipped cream which can be flavored with vanilla, rum or orange liqueur if desired. The whipped cream is swirled with an emerald crème de menthe sauce. You may also use curaçao in the sauce for a Caribbean blue effect. If you prefer to serve the fruit without the sauce, we recommend preparing a light coulis made with freshly chopped mint.

1. Scoop the fruit into balls using a melon baller.

2. Whip the cream until it forms soft peaks, then incorporate the sugar.

with Crème de Menthe Sauce

3. In a saucepan, warm the crème de menthe over low heat. Soften the gelatin sheets in cold water and stir them into the warm liqueur until dissolved. Allow the sauce to cool.

4. Build the multi-colored fruit cluster on a bed of whipped cream. Swirl lines of crème de menthe sauce into the whipped cream and top the cluster with a sprig of mint.

Kiwi, Litchi

For the sabayon:
8 egg yolks
⅔ cup/150 ml sugar syrup (see basic recipe)
3½ tbsp/50 ml orange liqueur
½ tsp curry powder
⅔ cup/150 ml whipping cream

2 kiwis
1 papaya
12 litchis

confectioners' sugar

Serves 4
Preparation time: 25 minutes
Cooking time: 30 minutes
Difficulty: ★

When we speak of *gratin* in cuisine, we refer to a baked dish in which a soft interior is topped by a crunchy crust. The contrast of textures brings out the delicate flavors of fruits or vegetables. Fruit gratins serve as excellent finales to family gatherings or small dinner parties. Generally speaking, gratins are prepared in oven-proof terra cotta baking dishes which can be brought directly to the table and served.

Our chef recommends preparing this dessert immediately before serving so that the fruit remains fresh and does not turn brown. If you choose to prepare the ingredients ahead of time, soak the fruit in a bit of orange liqueur to add flavor and keep it from turning brown.

Other fruits which may be used in this gratin include segments of citrus fruit such as oranges, mandarin oranges or pomelos. Lemons are not appropriate here because their sour flavor would overpower the rest.

Serve the Kiwi, Litchi and Papaya Gratin hot from the oven accompanied by a citrus sorbet.

1. In a saucepan over low heat, whisk together the yolks, sugar syrup and orange liqueur for 15 minutes until the mixture is creamy yellow. Add the curry powder and allow the mixture to cool. During this time, whip the cream to soft peaks and fold it into the egg mixture.

2. Spoon the sabayon onto the plate and spread into a thick layer.

and Papaya Gratin

3. Slice the kiwi into rounds and cut the papaya into thin strips. Halve the litchis and remove their pits. Arrange the fruit decoratively over the sabayon.

4. Broil the fruit and sabayon for 5 to 6 minutes in a 450 °F/250 °C oven until the top is evenly browned. Sprinkle with confectioners' sugar and serve hot.

Martinique

4 bananas
4 oranges
2 mangos
1 pineapple
4 passion fruit
1 star fruit
¾ cup/200 ml white rum

For the sabayon:
8 egg yolks
⅔ cup/150 ml sugar cane syrup
10 tbsp/150 g crème fraîche

Serves	4
Preparation time:	20 minutes
Cooking time:	20 minutes
Chilling time:	30 minutes
Difficulty:	★

The quality of the fruit chosen for this dessert is the secret to its success: Select bananas, mangos and a pineapple which are ripe yet firm and juicy oranges. Slice the fruit thin enough to be cut and eaten with a spoon.

Segment the oranges carefully, removing all skin and pith so that the oranges will cook better and be easier to digest. Feel free to substitute other fruits for the ones given here and add vanilla for flavor, if desired. Once sliced, refrigerate all of the fruits and drain them well before preparing the dessert.

To avoid overcooking the sabayon mousse, our chef recommends poaching it in a double-boiler over low heat until it begins to thicken, then gradually raising the heat until the sabayon reaches 160 °F/80 °C.

Adding the crème fraîche is the last step in assembling the sabayon. Lay the fruit in a decorative pattern on top of the sabayon, alternating colors. Broil the gratin and garnish with a slice of star fruit. Serve warm drizzled with passion fruit pulp.

1. Carefully peel the fruits, slice the bananas, mangos and oranges into thin strips, and segment the oranges. (The passion fruit and star fruit will be used to garnish the gratin and should be cut just before serving).

2. Marinate the fruit in the rum and chill for 30 minutes. Reserve 3½ tbsp/100 ml rum for the sabayon.

Sunday Gratin

3. While the fruit is marinating, make the sabayon: Whisk the yolks until they are light yellow. Add the cane syrup and 3½ tbsp/100 ml rum. Poach the mixture in a saucepan over low heat until it thickens into a creamy mousse. Cool the mixture and add the crème fraîche.

4. Spread the sabayon mixture over the bottom of an oven-proof plate. Arrange the fruit on top of the sabayon in a decorative pattern. Broil at high heat until the top is brown, then drizzle the gratin with passion fruit pulp and place a slice of star fruit in the center as a garnish.

Honey-Almond

For the filling:
2 cups/350 g ground almonds
¾ c/175 g sugar
1 tsp cinnamon
zest of 1 orange
2 eggs

1 package *feuilles de brick*
1 egg white
oil for frying
7 oz/200 g honey
3½ tbsp/50 ml aged rum

Serves	*4*
Preparation time:	*30 minutes*
Cooking time:	*20 minutes*
Difficulty:	★ ★

These almond-filled, honey-coated "havanas" will sweeten the end of any light meal or small dinner party without the health hazards contained by their tobacco-filled namesakes.

When following this recipe, it is important to use fresh *feuilles de brick*. Remove them from the package just before use to keep them from drying out and cracking. Here, the feuilles de brick are rolled into cigars; they may also be folded into triangles to different effect. Walnuts or hazelnuts can be used to replace the almonds in the filling. Whatever nut you choose, we recommend chopping rather than grinding them into a fine powder to keep the filling of the havanas crunchy.

As an alternative to frying, the havanas can be baked in the oven for a lighter, crispier result. Our chef recommends dipping the havanas into the honey immediately after frying and draining (or baking them). The havanas will then absorb the honey mixture better and retain a light coating of the sauce.

Select an amber-colored, liquid honey. We especially recommend orange-flower, locust or thousand-flower honeys which go well with the almond center of this dessert. You may intensify the flavor of the honey sauce by adding the zest of an orange or a few drops of orange-flower water.

1. To prepare the cigar filling, stir together the ground almonds, sugar, cinnamon and orange zest. Whisk in the eggs.

2. Cut the feuille de brick diagonally to make two semi-circles, place a spoonful of almond filling in the center of each, then fold the sides to the center as if you were making an envelope. Roll the cigar from the bottom up and seal the edges together with egg white.

Havanas

3. Drop the cigars one at a time into the hot oil and fry until golden brown, turning them from time to time to insure they cook evenly. Drain on paper towels.

4. In a saucepan, warm the honey with the rum. Dip the cigars in the honey sauce one by one to coat each cigar well with the honey mixture. Place the cigars on a small plate and serve hot.

Granada

12 egg whites
1¼ cups/300 g sugar
4 gooseberries
2 kiwis
1 pomegranate

For the fruit custard:
2 cups/500 ml milk
6 egg yolks
½ cup/120 g sugar
juice of 1 orange
2 passion fruit

Serves	*4*
Preparation time:	*35 minutes*
Cooking time:	*15 minutes*
Difficulty:	*★*

The Grenada Isles in the French Antilles are the stuff of dreams for those enamored of the exotic. Elegant and appetizing, these Floating Islands named in honor of the beautiful Isles will delight the palate of any gourmet.

Select fruit that is firm to the touch so that it will hold its shape when scooped into balls with a melon-baller. Vary the flavors of this dessert by using other tropical fruits and a dash of liqueur, if desired (rum, passion fruit liqueur, Triple Sec…).

To poach the meringue, bring the milk to a boil. Shape the meringue on a slotted spoon which can then be lowered directly into the hot milk. To keep the meringue from falling, do not exceed the stated time for poaching. Over-cooking will cause the meringue to flatten and look dull rather than shiny.

Drain the meringues on a clean, dry towel or paper towel and reserve the milk for the custard. Once the custard has thickened, add the reduced orange juice and passion fruit for flavor.

Garnish the meringue with the fruit balls arranged decoratively over the top and sides. Coat the bottom of a plate with the custard and place the meringue island in the center. Sprinkle with small bits of spun sugar, if desired.

1. Beat the egg whites with the sugar until they form a stiff meringue. Shape the islands on a slotted spoon with a scraper.

2. Slide the meringues into a saucepan full of boiling milk. Cook for 3 to 4 minutes on each side, them remove them from the milk and drain on a clean towel. Reserve the milk for the custard.

Floating Islands

3. Using a circular motion, scoop the fruit into balls using a melon-baller. Seed the pomegranate.

4. Bring the reserved milk to a boil. Whisk the eggs and sugar together, add the orange juice and passion fruit pulp to the boiling milk, then pour it over the egg mixture, stirring briskly. Return the custard to the saucepan and poach until thick. Serve the custard with the fruit-studded meringue.

Flambéed Savanna Mango

2 large mangos
2 tbsp/30 g brown sugar
2 tbsp/30 g butter
⅔ cup/150 ml scotch whisky
juice of 1 orange
1 tsp/10 g grated ginger
3 Jamaican peppercorns

Serves	*4*
Preparation time:	*10 minutes*
Cooking time:	*15 minutes*
Difficulty:	★

This recipe hearkens back to the colonial heritage of the Caribbean Islands. Our chef has chosen Scotch whisky in homage to the sailors from the British Isles who first colonized the Caribbean. Scotch is made with rye, barley, oats or corn and distilled with peat. Each Scotch varies according to the grain used, but all have the rich, mellow flavor that comes from months of fermentation in oak barrels. Our Flambeed Savanna Mangos are our "Here, here!" to all whisky lovers.

The mango is roasted with brown sugar and sweet butter. A sauce is made by deglazing the pan with the orange juice Scotch, fresh ginger and cinnamon (if desired).

To accommodate ginger fans, this dessert may be served with a ginger sorbet: Grate 3½ oz/50 g of ginger. Add the juice of 2 lemons, 2 cups/500 ml of sugar syrup and ¾ cup/200 ml of water. Turn in an ice cream machine and store in the freezer.

For added effect to this simple dessert, switch off all lights before serving and flambé the mangos at the table with whisky or rum. This step must be done with caution: Alcohol fumes can be overpowering.

1. Slice the lobes of the mango from the pit and cut them lengthwise into thick strips.

2. Place the mangos in a baking dish, sprinkle with brown sugar, dot with butter and bake for 15 minutes at 350 °F/180 °C.

with Scotch Sauce

3. Deglaze the baking dish with the Scotch and orange juice. Add the grated ginger and the Jamaican peppercorns.

4. Fan the mango slices out on the plate and coat them with the sauce. Serve warm.

Polynesian

For the choux pastry:
1 cup/250 ml water
½ cup/120 ml milk
½ cup plus 2 tbsp/150 g butter
a pinch of salt
1¾ cup plus 2 tbsp/225 g flour
5 eggs
1 egg yolk

For the chocolate sauce:
5¼ oz/150 g bittersweet chocolate
1¼ cup/300 ml sugar syrup (see
    basic recipe)

For the vanilla ice cream:
2 cups/500 ml milk
6½ tbsp/100 g sugar
6 egg yolks
5 vanilla beans, scraped

Serves	4
Preparation time:	1 hour
Cooking time:	30 minutes
Chilling time:	20 minutes
Difficulty:	★ ★

The choux pastry is the essential element in this dessert: It must be light and crisp after baking to stand up to the moisture in the ice cream and banana.

To make the eclairs, bring the milk and water to a boil. Away from the heat, add the sifted flour and stir with a wooden spoon until all of the flour is incorporated and the dough has no lumps. Dry the dough over the heat for one to two minutes to allow any excess moisture to evaporate, then remove it from the saucepan to a mixing bowl. Stir in the eggs one by one with a wooden spoon. The resulting dough will be shiny and fluid enough to stream in a ribbon from the spoon.

Using a pastry bag fitted with a round tip, pipe the eclairs onto a sheet of parchment paper. Flatten them with the back of a fork to release any air bubbles, then brush them with the egg yolk diluted with a little water.

While the eclairs are baking, roast the bananas in a sauté pan or in the oven. Thin the chocolate sauce with a teaspoon of sugar syrup or milk, if necessary.

Once the eclairs have cooled, cut them in half. Spread a layer of vanilla ice cream on the bottom half of the eclair and top with half of a caramelized banana. Close the eclair, and drizzle the top with chocolate sauce.

Our chef suggests serving this Polynesian eclair with an espresso sauce.

1. In a saucepan, bring the water, milk, butter and salt to a boil. Remove from the heat and stir in the flour.

2. Place the choux dough in a bowl. Add the eggs to the dough one by one. Slice the bananas lengthwise, then caramelize the slices in a sauté pan with a small amount of sugar.

Eclair

3. Melt the chocolate in a double boiler. Warm the sugar syrup slightly then add to the chocolate to make a shiny, smooth sauce. Using a pastry bag, pipe the eclairs onto parchment paper.

4. Split the eclairs in half, and spread the bottom of each with vanilla ice cream. Place a slice of caramelized banana on the ice cream and finish with the top of the eclair. Garnish with warm chocolate sauce and serve.

Island Orchid

1 package phyllo dough
6½ tbsp/100 g butter
6½ tbsp/100 g sugar or brown sugar
1 star fruit
1 papaya
1 banana
½ pineapple
7 oz/200 g fromage blanc

6½ tbsp/100 g sugar
1 vanilla bean

For the papaya sauce:
½ papaya
6½ tbsp/100 ml sugar syrup (see basic recipe)

Serves 4
Preparation time: 30 minutes
Cooking time: 10 minutes
Difficulty: ★ ★

The orchid is a remarkable flower which flourishes in tropical climates. There are over 15,000 species of orchid, including the vanilla orchid, which produces the vanilla beans used to flavor our succulent desserts. Our chef has shaped the phyllo dough in this dessert to look like a tropical flower.

When preparing the phyllo dough, brush it with melted butter and sprinkle it generously with sugar. This will give the phyllo a crunchy caramelized flavor and texture beyond compare. For a uniformly shaped flower, lay the phyllo strips in a blini pan or another mold of the same size. To reinforce the bottom of the flower, fold a strip of phyllo into quarters and place it in the center of the mold before adding the filling.

Marinating the chopped fruit in 6½ tbsp/100 ml of white or dark rum before stirring it into the fromage blanc will bring out its natural flavor. Cut the vanilla bean in half and scrape the beans into the fromage blanc. Delicately stir the fruit and vanilla into the fromage blanc. For the fruit, you may alternatively use mangos, soursops, jack fruit or a number of other exotic fruits on the market according to the season and availability.

1. Cut the phyllo dough into 2½ in/6 cm strips. Brush the strips with melted butter and sprinkle with granulated or brown sugar. Dice the fruit.

2. Crisscross strips of phyllo dough in the mold, allowing any excess to lap over the sides. Stir together the fruit, the fromage blanc, 6½ tbsp/100 g of sugar and the vanilla bean. Fill the mold with the fromage blanc mixture.

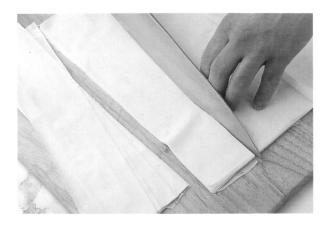

Dessert

3. Fold the edges of the phyllo dough up and over the fromage blanc filling and shape the edges to look like a flower. Bake in a hot oven (400 °F/190 °C) for 10 minutes.

4. To make the papaya sauce, blend the papaya with the sugar syrup and warm in a saucepan. Place the orchid in the center of the plate, garnish with the warm sauce and serve.

Kanakie

8¾ oz/250 g sweet dough (see
   basic recipe)
2 guavas

For the egg custard:
2 cups/500 ml whipping cream
½ cup/125 g sugar
2 eggs
1 vanilla bean

Serves   4
Preparation time: 20 minutes
Cooking time: 25 minutes
Difficulty: ★ ★

Tart and flavorful, guavas contain large black seeds which are hard but can be eaten. Guavas, which have a high nutritional value, are eaten plain or made into juice in tropical countries. Guava cocktails, ice creams and jellies are common, as are guavas canned in syrup.

When shaping the sweet dough for this Kanakie tart, let the excess dough lap over the edge of the tart form in order to keep the dough from shrinking in the oven. Another way to prevent shrinkage is to prebake the tart circles before filling them: Place aluminum foil over the dough and fill the shells with beans or rice to hold the dough in place while baking. Once the tart shells are partially baked, remove the beans, fill the shells with custard and finish baking. We suggest preheating the oven well to ensure even baking.

While the tarts are are in the oven, check them through the window of the oven to make sure the custard filling does not overflow, but avoid opening the oven door if possible. Once cooled, trim the excess dough with a serrated knife, unmold the tarts and serve warm.

A pâte sablée (see basic recipe) or a less sweet dough may also be used in this dessert. The tarts can be filled with bread fruit, mangos or other firm-fleshed exotic fruit instead of guavas. Sprinkle the tarts with powdered sugar before serving and garnish with a slice of guava.

1. Press the sweet dough into the tart forms without puncturing it. Allow any excess dough to lap over the sides.

2. Peel and seed the guavas. Slice them thinly and arrange the slices on the bottom of the tart.

Tart

3. To make the egg custard, whisk together the whipping cream, sugar, eggs and vanilla bean.

4. Pour the custard over the sliced guavas. Bake at 350 °F/180 °C for 25 minutes. Remove the excess dough from the sides, unmold and serve warm.

For the pomelo mousse:
juice of 1 pomelo
½ cup plus 2 tbsp/150 g sugar
5 sheets of gelatin
6½ tbsp/100 ml champagne
2 cups/500 ml whipping cream

For the caramel sauce:
6½ tbsp milk
3½ tbsp/50 g sugar
3½ tbsp/50 ml water

For the garnish:
pomelo segments
½ oz/10 g candied pomelo zests

Serves	4
Preparation time:	30 minutes
Cooking time:	10 minutes
Chilling time:	2 hours
Difficulty:	★ ★

La Soufrière, the active volcano on the island of Guadeloupe, first erupted between 1250 and 1550, probably before the arrival of Columbus in the Caribbean. The first recorded eruption, complete with explosions and flying ash, occurred in 1797. Other eruptions in 1956 and 1976 shook the island politically more than geologically. Today, La Soufrière is a quiet presence which no longer troubles the inhabitants of Guadeloupe.

Our chef has created this volcano treat for your pleasure and hopes the only eruptions it will cause will be those of the guests at your table when they taste this dessert made with pomelos—a dessert to end a meal with a bang.

The pomelo belongs to the same citrus family as the grapefruit. Inside its thick, pithy skin is a tart, juicy fruit which is rich in vitamins A and C. We have used every element of the pomelo in this dessert: juice for the mousse, segments and candied zest for the garnish. This dessert should be prepared just before serving so that the fruit segments stay fresh and the juice in the mousse retains its vitamins.

1. In a saucepan, heat the pomelo juice with the sugar. Soften the gelatin in cold water and add to the warm juice mixture. Remove from the heat and add the champagne.

2. Allow the juice mixture to cool. Whip the cream, add ¼ of the whipped cream to the juice mixture. Pour the juice over the rest of the whipped cream while stirring briskly.

Soufrière

3. Spoon the pomelo mousse into a cone-shaped mold. Chill for 2 hours until set. To unmold, dip the cone in hot water for a few seconds to loosen the mousse.

4. In a saucepan, boil the sugar and water until a dark caramel forms. Warm the milk and add it to the caramel to stop the sugar from cooking further. Place the pomelo mousse on the plate with the pomelo segments surrounding it. Garnish with the caramel sauce and several candied zests for decoration.

Chocolate

8¾ oz/250 g high quality dark chocolate
¾ cup plus 1 tbsp/200 g butter
½ cup strong coffee or espresso
8 eggs, separated
1¼ cups/300 g sugar
⅔ cup/80 g unsweetened cocoa

Serves	4
Preparation time:	30 minutes
Cooking time:	15 minutes
Difficulty:	★

To recognize good chocolate, look for a shiny and dark brown surface. It should break without crumbling into clean, matte pieces. The secret to the rich chocolate flavor of this dessert is the balance between the sweet, dark chocolate and the bitter, unsweetened cocoa powder.

The beaten egg whites in this torte recipe keep the cake moist. Beat them into stiff peaks with an electric mixer, then add the sugar to consolidate the meringue and keep it from falling. Beat the meringue two to three minutes longer to obtain a shiny, smooth product which will remain airy and stiff when added to the chocolate.

Whisk the egg yolks and the butter into the melted chocolate. Fold a small amount of meringue into the chocolate to lighten the mixture, then carefully incorporate the rest of the meringue. Our chef suggests baking the torte in two stages: first, fill the buttered and floured molds only halfway and bake for five minutes. Remove the tortes from the oven, add the rest of the chocolate mixture and bake for five more minutes. Unmold the tortes while still warm and sprinkle them with powdered sugar and cocoa powder.

Use a high-quality dark chocolate of your choice. Instant coffee diluted in water may be used instead of espresso or strong coffee. Ground almonds or walnuts also make excellent additions to the recipe. Serve with a crème anglaise custard or coffee sauce, if desired.

1. Break the chocolate into small pieces and melt it in a double boiler. Stir in the melted butter and espresso.

2. Separate the eggs. Beat the egg whites with the sugar to make the meringue, then fold in the cocoa powder. Pour the chocolate mixture into a bowl and stir in the egg yolks. Gently fold the meringue into the chocolate mixture with a spatula.

Oblivion Torte

3. Grease the tart rings with softened butter. Line each ring with a strip of parchment paper and place them on a baking sheet lined with parchment paper.

4. Fill the tart circles half-way with the torte batter and bake for 5 minutes at 350 °F/180 °C. Add the rest of the batter to the circles and bake until set. Serve warm.

Aunt Lucie's

For the cannoli dough:
2 cups/250 g flour
1 tsp salt
1 tsp sugar
1 egg
3½ tbsp/50 g butter, melted
6½ tbsp/100 ml orange liqueur
oil for frying

For the espresso cream filling:
5¼ oz/150 g fromage blanc
2 tbsp espresso or strong coffee
1¾ oz/50 g confectioners' sugar

For the combava/lime cream filling:
5¼ oz/150 g fromage blanc
1¾ oz/50 g confectioners' sugar
juice of 1 combava or lime

Serves	*4*
Preparation time:	*40 minutes*
Cooking time:	*15 minutes*
Resting time:	*24 hours*
Difficulty:	★ ★

Aunt Lucie has always been proud of her Italian heritage: Here she gives us her recipe for Creole cannoli. Traditional cannoli call for a cylinder of fried dough filled with ricotta cheese and candied fruit. Our chef has adapted this recipe to use a tangy *f*romage blanc flavored with combava zest and espresso.

Prepare the cannoli dough and allow it to rest overnight. Handle the dough as little as possible to keep it from becoming too elastic. Roll out the dough into 4 in/10 cm circles. Wrap the dough around a bamboo stick or the handle of a wooden spoon and dip the stick into the hot oil. Once it has begun to fry, the cannoli will expand and come off of the stick or spoon easily. Drain the cannoli well on paper towels.

Orange or lime zest may be used in place of the combava limes to flavor the citrus cream. Chocolate and vanilla make excellent substitutes for the coffee in the cream filling. Use a pastry bag fitted with a small fluted pastry tip to fill the cannoli.

We suggest serving this dessert accompanied by an espresso sauce. For the espresso sauce, heat 6½ tbsp/100 ml of whipping cream with 1 tsp instant coffee. Whisk an egg yolk together with 2 tsp sugar, then whisk the espresso cream into the egg mixture, return the custard to the saucepan and poach until thick

Bravo, Aunt Lucie, for this crowd-pleasing dessert.

1. Prepare the cannoli dough a day ahead: Stir together the flour, salt and sugar. Add the egg, melted butter and orange liqueur and mix until a moist dough forms.

2. Roll out the cannoli dough very thin. Cut circles out of the dough with a round cutter, wrap the cannoli circles around a bamboo stick and fry in hot oil.

Creole Cannoli

3. For the combava lime cream, mix together the fromage blanc, sugar and combava lime zest. Whip the fromage blanc mixture lightly until it is smooth and creamy.

4. For the espresso cream, stir the coffee and sugar into 1 tbsp of the fromage blanc. Whisk in the rest of the fromage blanc. Fill one end of the cannoli with the combava lime cream and the other end with the espresso cream. Serve garnished with an espresso sauce and a wedge of combava lime, if desired.

For the pastry cream:
6 egg yolks
6½ tbsp/100 g sugar
1 cup/120 g flour
2 cups/500 ml coconut milk
6½ tbsp/100 ml whipping cream
6½ tbsp/100 ml rum

For the choux pastry (see basic recipe)**:**
1 cup/250 ml water
6½ tbsp/100 g butter

1 tsp/5 g sugar
½ tsp/2 g salt
1¼ cups flour
5 eggs

For the garnish:
1½ oz/40 g grated coconut

Serves	*4*
Preparation time:	*1 hour*
Cooking time:	*25 minutes*
Difficulty:	★ ★

As the story goes, the famous Paris-Brest pastry was invented in the last century by a baker who could watch the Paris-Brest bicycle race from his shop window. In honor of the race, he formed the dough into a round, doughnut shape to look like the wheels of a bicycle. Since the Paris-Brest first appeared, other variations have followed including the Paris-Nice. Here we introduce yet another: The Paris-Basse-Terre, named for the direct flights that now reach from the French capital to the old town in Guadeloupe.

Basse-Terre was founded in 1643, at the beginning of French colonization of Guadeloupe. Though smaller and less active than Pointe-à-Pitre, Basse-Terre has remained the capital of the island and is home to a well-known weather observatory.

A light, crisp choux pastry is the secret to this recipe's success. The Paris-Basse-Terre should be assembled the day it is served, because the pastry gets soggy when it is in prolonged contact with the cream. The baked pastry circles can be baked ahead of time, frozen, and defrosted as needed.

1. For the pastry cream, whisk together the egg yolks, sugar and flour. In a saucepan. Bring the coconut milk to a boil, then pour it over the yolk mixture, whisking constantly. Heat the coconut pastry cream gently for about 6 minutes. Once the pastry cream has cooled, fold in the whipped cream and the rum to make a light custard.

2. Pipe the choux pastry into circles using a pastry bag fitted with a round tip. Brush the tops with egg yolk and bake for 25 minutes at 375 °F/190 °C. Remove from the baking sheet and cool.

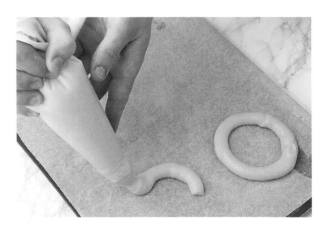

Basse-Terre

3. Slice the circles horizontally with a serrated knife.

4. Garnish the bottom half of the rounds with the light coconut cream. Place the tops on the cream and sprinkle with grated coconut.

Tangy Passion

¾ cup/175 ml egg whites
3½ tbsp/50 g sugar
1⅔ cups ground almonds
8¾ oz confectioners' sugar

For the passion fruit cream filling:
1 cup/250 ml passion fruit concentrate
4 tsp sugar

2 sheets gelatin
2 cups/500 ml whipping cream

For the garnish:
1 passion fruit for decoration

Serves	4
Preparation time:	1 hour
Cooking time:	35 minutes
Resting time:	30 minutes
Chilling time:	15 minutes
Difficulty:	★ ★

Macaroons are small, round cookies, crunchy on the outside, soft and chewy on the inside, traditionally made with chopped almonds. Italian confections which are said to have originated in Venice, macaroons are at least hundreds, if not thousands, of years old. Although it is generally accepted that macaroons were created during the Renaissance, some believe they were first made by an Italian monastery in 791, hence the now archaic name for them: "Monk's Navels."

The secret to beautiful macaroons is a delicate hand in incorporating the egg whites into the almond and sugar mixture. Fold the egg whites in gently with a spatula or wooden spoon to keep them from breaking. Using a pastry bag fitted with a round tip, pipe the macaroons onto a baking sheet lined with parchment paper. Drop the baking sheet flat onto the counter two or three times to even out the macaroon batter and eliminate any imperfections or air bubbles.

Once they are piped, let the macaroons sit for half an hour before baking to allow them to dry out and develop a crust. For perfect macaroons, bake for ten minutes at 350 °C/180 °F, open the oven door for several minutes to lower the temperature, then continue baking at 275 °F/140 °C for another 15 to 20 minutes.

Serve the macaroons with a crème anglaise custard drizzled with passion fruit pulp, and garnish with miniature apple quarters, if desired.

1. For the macaroon batter, beat the egg whites with the sugar. Sift together the almond flour and confectioners' sugar, and fold into the sweetened egg whites. Pipe the batter onto a baking sheet lined with parchment paper.

2. Bake the macaroons twice for approximately 30 minutes, first at 350 °F/180 °C, then at 275 °F/140 °C. To remove the macaroons from the parchment paper, pour a small amount of water onto the baking sheet under the paper. The moisture and humidity will soften the bottoms of the baked macaroons and make them easier to remove.

Fruit Macaroons

3. To make the cream filling, heat the passion fruit juice with the sugar. Soften the gelatin sheets in cold water and add to the warm juice. Whip the cream and fold it into the cooled fruit juice using a spatula or wooden spoon with a circular motion from the bottom of the bowl to the top, making sure no whipped cream remains at the bottom. Refrigerate the cream mixture for 15 minutes.

4. Fill the macaroons with the passion fruit cream using a pastry bag fitted with a fluted tip. Place the macaroons on the plate and garnish with crème anglaise and drops of passion fruit pulp.

Paradisio

For the meringue:
5 egg whites
½ cup/125 g sugar

For the Asian pear cream:
juice of 3 Asian pears
½ cup/125 g sugar
2 cups/500 ml whipping cream

16 strawberries
2 kiwis
½ dragon fruit
8 gooseberries
1 small star fruit

Serves	*4*
Preparation time:	*30 minutes*
Cooking time:	*1 hour 30 minutes*
Difficulty:	★

Our Meringue Paradisio is an easy-to-prepare dessert which will provide a stunning finish to a dinner party. For this recipe, our chef has chosen the mild flavor of Asian pears to go with the more distinctive flavors and colors of strawberries, gooseberries, kiwis and dragon fruit. For a citrus tang, the juice of one orange may be added to the Asian pear cream.

Native to Central America and Australia, Asian pears, have a soft, sweet flesh which is full of flavor though not sour or tart. Asian pears are nonetheless high in vitamin C and can be served fresh or in sorbets. Unlike common pears, Asian pears grow on vines and belong to the same family as passion fruit.

Good strawberries, imported from tropical regions when not in season, can now be found the year round. Select whole, ripe strawberries whose stems and leaves are intact and whose skin appears dry. Avoid washing them if possible as they lose much of their flavor. Instead, wipe off any dirt with a damp cloth.

Slice all of the fruit carefully: Cut the strawberries into quarters, the kiwi into eight slices length-wise, the gooseberries in half and the star fruit into four slices (if desired). Scoop balls out of the dragon fruit with a melon baller.

Meringues vary widely in texture from moist and chewy to crisp and light according to the length of time they are baked or dried. Here we recommend finding a happy medium between the two textures: not too moist but not too brittle.

1. To make the meringue, beat the egg whites with the sugar until stiff.

2. Using a pastry bag fitted with a round tip, pipe spirals of meringue onto a baking sheet lined with parchment paper. Bake in a warm oven, (200 °F/90 °C) for 1½ hours so that the meringues dry but remain white.

Meringue

3. To make the cream, reduce the Asian pear juice by boiling it for 10 minutes with the sugar and allow to cool. During this time, whip the cream and fold it into the reduced juice with a spatula. Slice all of the fruit.

4. Pipe a dome of the Asian pear cream onto the meringue. Decorate the cream with the sliced fruit and serve, garnished with drops of Asian pear or strawberry coulis, if desired.

For 20 tart shells:
7 oz/200 g sweet dough (see basic recipe)

For the chocolate tarts:
6½ tbsp/100 ml milk
3½ tbsp/50 ml whipping cream
4½ oz bittersweet chocolate
4 tsp/20 ml rum
1 egg

For the ginger-vanilla tarts:
3½ oz/100 g pastry cream (see basic recipe)
2 vanilla beans
½ oz/10 g candied ginger

For the cappuccino tarts:
1 cup/250 ml milk
3 tsp instant coffee
3 egg yolks
8 tsp/40 g sugar
¼ cup/30 g flour

Serves	4
Preparation time:	45 minutes
Cooking time:	20 minutes
Difficulty:	★ ★

The fruit of the cocoa tree is harvested ripe and the outer rind is discarded. The beans at the center of the fruit are dried and fermented in the sun and then ground into paste which, in tropical countries, is formed into large cylinders of raw chocolate which are sold at outdoor markets. The raw chocolate is grated and melted in milk to make a chocolate drink served warm or cold. Because these raw chocolate cylinders are hard to find outside tropical regions, our recipe for chocolate tarts calls for sweetened, refined chocolate, the most common form of chocolate in Western countries which is sold in bars or chips.

The three tart *petits fours* are made with a delicate sweet crust. The secret to a light, crisp, delicious sweet dough is to handle the it as little as possible. Kneading the dough will make it too elastic and make the crust dry and hard. Mix the ingredients for the sweet dough together quickly with the tips of your fingers. Shape the dough into a ball and mash it with the palm of your hand to smooth out any lumps in the dough.

For best results, chill the dough for two hours or overnight wrapped in a clean dishtowel or plastic wrap. Roll the dough out evenly on a floured surface. The tart shells should be baked until they just begin to turn brown. For the chocolate tarts: Bake the filled tarts a second time at 200 °F/90 °C maximum. The low temperature allows the chocolate filling to set without browning the sweet dough or causing it to crack.

Serve these "Arawak Trail Petits Fours" as an afternoon treat with hot chocolate, cappuccino or vanilla-flavored tea.

1. Roll the sweet dough to a thickness of ¹⁄₁₆ inch/2 mm cut into circles with a cutter. Bake the shells for 5 minutes at 350 °F/180 °C.

2. For the chocolate tarts, bring the milk and cream to a boil. Break the chocolate into small pieces and pour the boiling milk over it, stirring until all of the chocolate has melted. Whisk in the egg and the rum, fill the tart shells and bake for 10 minutes at 200°F/90 °C.

Petits Fours

3. For the vanilla-ginger tarts, whip the cream with the seeds of the vanilla beans. Dice the candied ginger. Fold the whipped cream and candied ginger into the pastry cream, pipe the cream into the tart shells and garnish with the remaining vanilla beans.

4. For the coffee cream, bring the milk to a boil with the instant coffee. Whisk together the egg yolks, sugar and flour. Pour the milk over the egg mixture, whisking constantly. Return the mixture to the saucepan and poach for 5 minutes, stirring constantly. Pour the cream into the tart shells and cool. Garnish with whipped cream, cocoa powder and a coffee bean, if desired.

Passion-Papaya

10½ oz/300 g puff pastry (see
   basic recipe)
3½ oz confectioners' sugar
2 papayas

For the orange coulis:
2 oranges
3½ tbsp/50 g butter
4 tsp/20 g sugar
6½ tbsp/100 ml Triple Sec

For the passion fruit cream:
⅔ cup/150 ml passion fruit juice
3½ tbsp/50 ml whipped cream (see
   basic recipe)
2 tbsp/30 g sugar

Serves	*4*
Preparation time:	*1 hour*
Cooking time:	*25 minutes*
Chilling time:	*15 minutes*
Difficulty:	*★ ★ ★*

For French children and adults alike, the mention of *mille-feuille* brings to mind the thin dusting of confectioners' sugar the traditional pastry, consisting of layers of puff pastry and pastry cream, is given. The fine sugar coating takes to the air at the first breath of wind—indeed, most French children have been dusted at least once by their playful companions!

Passion fruit and papaya make a surprisingly tangy combination in this version of millefeuille, but they may be replaced by strawberries or mangos. Pastry cream may be used as a filling instead of the passion fruit cream for a more traditional millefeuille. Grapefruit is another option for the citrus coulis.

Be careful when baking the puff pastry: Over-cooked puff pastry can taste bitter. To form the pastry into 12 identical rectangles, cut a piece of cardboard 2x4 in/5x10 cm. Using the piece of cardboard as a pattern, cut the puff pastry in one swift movement of the knife while the pastry is still hot.

The whipped cream should be folded into the passion fruit juice delicately with a spatula. Use a circular motion with the spatula, moving from the bottom of the bowl to the top of the mixture to aerate the cream and keep it from falling. Drain the papaya slices well before placing them in the millefeuille so that their juice does not make the pastry soggy.

To decorate the millefeuille, place a metal spatula diagonally over the last layer of puff pastry. Using a small strainer or shaker, sprinkle the pastry lightly with the confectioners' sugar to keep it from lumping.

1. Roll out the puff pastry to ⅛ in/2 mm thickness. Prick the dough with a fork, and sprinkle with confectioners' sugar. Weigh it down with a rack and bake in a hot oven (400 °F/200 °C) for 10 to 15 minutes.

2. Cut the puff pastry into rectangles while still hot; slice the papaya lengthwise. For the orange coulis, peel and chop the oranges, and sauté the orange pulp with the butter and sugar. Once the oranges have cooked, but not caramelized, add the Triple Sec.

Millefeuille

3. Reduce the passion fruit juice with the sugar over low heat, and allow to cool. With a rubber spatula, fold in the whipped cream. Refrigerate the passion fruit cream for 15 minutes.

4. Spread a layer of passion fruit cream on the first rectangle of puff pastry. Place the sliced papaya on top of the cream, cover with a second rectangle of pastry and repeat, ending with a third rectangle of puff pastry. Sprinkle with confectioners' sugar and serve.

Pina Colada

For the coconut dacquoise:
5 egg whites
5 tsp/25 g granulated sugar
4½ oz/125 g confectioners' sugar
3½ oz/100 g grated coconut

For the coconut sorbet:
¾ cup/200 ml coconut milk
¾ cup/200 ml milk
1¼ cup/300 ml syrup (see basic recipe)
2 tsp/10 ml rum
1¾ oz/50 g unsweetened grated coconut

Serves   4
Preparation time: 45 minutes
Cooking time: 20 minutes
Freezing time: 40 minutes
Difficulty: ★ ★ ★

For the pina colada sauce:
6½ tbsp/100 ml pineapple juice
6½ tbsp/100 ml coconut milk
6½ tbsp/100 ml dark rum

For the Italian meringue:
4 egg whites
½ cup plus 2 tbsp/150 g sugar
⅔ cup/150 ml water

For the garnish:
1 passion fruit
slivered almonds
dried pineapple chips

What makes this baked Alaska so special is the combination of cold ice cream interior with hot Italian meringue on the outside. It is sure to delight gourmets and simple food lovers alike.

The pina colada cocktail is a delicious combination of pineapple juice, coconut and rum. Here we have heated the pina colada in the microwave for a warm sauce to accompany the baked Alaska. If the pina colada sauce seems too thin, add one teaspoon of cornstarch diluted in a little water. Because the pina colada is so sweet, we recommend adding tart passion fruit pulp to the sauce to even out the flavors of the dessert.

To save time, you may use store-bought coconut sorbet. If you have the time, our chef has provided a recipe for homemade coconut sorbet. Other ice cream and sorbet flavors may be used in this baked Alaska recipe.

The sponge cake generally used in a Baked Alaska has been replaced here by a crisper dacquoise for a different texture.

Decorate the baked Alaska with pineapple or banana chips, slivered almonds and pomegranate seeds for color. Serve the baked Alaska straight from the oven and flambee it with rum or orange liqueur, if desired.

1. For the dacquoise, beat the egg whites with the granulated sugar until they form stiff peaks. Stir together the confectioners' sugar and coconut, then fold the mixture into the meringue. Spread the batter ⅛ in/5 mm thick onto a baking sheet lined with parchment paper and place in a 350 °F/180 °C oven for 15 minutes.

2. For the coconut sorbet, whisk all of the ingredients together. Turn the mixture in an ice cream machine until it forms a smooth sorbet. To make the pina colada sauce, stir together the pineapple juice, the coconut milk and the dark rum.

Baked Alaska

3. Cut the cooled dacquoise into 4 identical rectangles. Place a quenelle of coconut sorbet in the center using a warmed spoon and put in the freezer for 40 minutes to set.

4. To make the Italian meringue, boil the sugar and water together to the soft ball stage (250 °F/120 °C). Beat the egg whites until stiff. Mix together the sugar and water and pour over the egg whites, beating the meringue until cool. Pipe the meringue over the coconut sorbet quenelles and place under the broiler until the meringue begins to brown and serve hot.

Strawberry-Banana

For the nougat:
3½ tbsp/50 g sugar
1 oz/25 ml corn syrup or glucose
4 egg whites
2 cups/500 ml whipping cream
5¼ oz/150 g candied fruit (papaya, pineapple, etc.)
5¼ oz/150 g black raisins or currants

For the garnish:
2 candied cherries
8 strips angelica
4 gooseberries

For the strawberry-banana sauce:
5 ripe strawberries
½ banana

Serves	4
Preparation time:	45 minutes
Cooking time:	10 minutes
Freezing time:	3 hours
Difficulty:	★ ★

Originally, the term "nougat" in cuisine referred to a dessert which contained at least 15 per cent fruit. Nougat as we now know it was first made with walnuts in Marseilles, France during the 16th century. Much later, when almond groves were planted in the south of France, Montelimar became the nougat capital, and Montelimar nougat, made with almonds, remains the most famous variety available today.

This recipe calls for glucose or corn syrup. Glucose acts as a stabilizer for the nougat and is essential to maintain a creamy consistency once the nougat is frozen. Chef's hint: Glucose and corn syrup are very sticky, so wet your hands in cold water before handling them and putting them on to boil.

The frozen nougat is garnished with a fresh strawberry-banana sauce. The fruits are blended but not cooked as cooking the strawberries would alter their taste. Blend the strawberries and the banana in a food processor or blender. Thin the mixture with sugar syrup or water if necessary. This sauce should be prepared immediately before serving so that the banana does not turn brown.

The frozen nougat may be made with any other available candied fruits: kiwis, orange zests, kumquats, angelica, citron, etc. Garnish the dessert with half of a candied cherry, slices of angelica and a gooseberry.

1. Bring the sugar, glucose and a little water to a boil. Cook to the soft ball stage (250 °F/120 °C).

2. Beat the egg whites until soft peaks form. Add the cooked sugar syrup and continue to beat until cool. During this time, whip the cream until firm peaks form. Fold the meringue into the whipped cream.

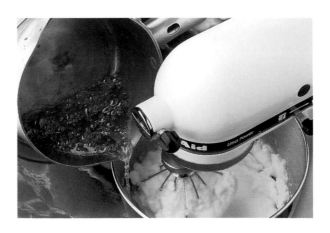

Nougat Glacé

3. Add the diced candied fruit and raisins to the whipped cream and meringue nougat. Fill an aluminum mold with the nougat and put in the freezer for 3 hours to set. Make the strawberry-banana sauce.

4. Unmold the nougat using a warmed knife. Smooth any rough edges. Coat the plate with the strawberry-banana sauce. Place the nougat in the center of the plate with the candied cherry, angelica slices and gooseberry as garnish. Serve cold.

Sesame Nougatine

2 mangoes
6½ tbsp/100 ml mango juice
1 pinch of curry powder
3½ tbsp/50 ml rum

For the nougatine:
3½ tbsp/50 ml water
6½ tbsp/100 g sugar
2½ oz/70 g sesame seeds
1 pinch of pepper

For the garnish:
a few fenugreek seeds

Serves   4
Preparation time: 1 hour
Cooking time: 15 minutes
Difficulty: ★ ★ ★

Mild white sesame seeds are a staple of Middle Eastern cooking. Sesame oil, an odorless, clear extraction from the seed, is also important. Sesame flour is frequently used to make flat breads or crepes. Tahini, or sesame paste, is made by grilling sesame seeds, grinding them and flavoring the paste with lemon juice. Tahini provides the base for a wide variety of condiments in Mediterranean and Middle Eastern Cuisine.

Our chefs have chosen to use the sesame seeds in a sweet rather than savory recipe. Sesame seeds take the place of finely chopped nuts in the nougatine, although hazelnuts, pistachios or almonds would also go well in this recipe.

When preparing the nougatine, pay close attention to the color of the caramel. If it is too light, it may not have enough flavor; but if the caramel is cooked too long and turns too dark it tends to become bitter. Grease the rolling pin and the parchment paper well with oil before rolling out the nougatine to prevent it from sticking. If the nougatine hardens before it is thin enough to shape, reheat it in a warm oven for 4 minutes to soften and continue to roll it out.

Nothing can compare to the taste of fresh, ripe mango. To select perfectly ripe mangos, choose fruit which is soft to the touch and has a smooth and taut skin.

1. To make the nougatine, prepare a caramel with the sugar and water. Add the sesame seeds and a pinch of fresh ground pepper. Stir together over low heat and spread onto an oiled sheet of parchment paper.

2. Grease the rolling pin and roll the nougatine into a thin sheet about 1 mm in thickness. Cut with a cutter or a knife, depending on the shape you choose for the dessert.

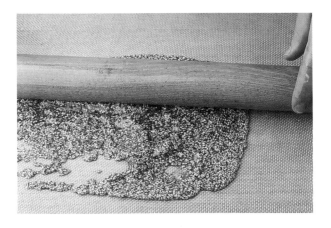

with Peppered Mangoes

3. Slice the mangos lengthwise. Place several strips on a round of nougatine, cover with a second round of nougatine and repeat. Finish with a third round of nougatine. Garnish as desired.

4. To make the curried mango coulis, warm the mango juice in a saucepan. Add the rum and curry powder. Swirl the sauce around the dessert and serve.

Antilles-Style

For the pistachio mousseline filling:
1¼ cup/200 g unsalted pistachios
½ vanilla bean
1 cup/250 ml milk
3 egg yolks
3½ tbsp/50 g sugar
¼ cup/30 g flour
6½ tbsp/100 g butter, softened
juice of 1 lime

For the nougatine:
1 cup/200 g sugar
6½ tbsp/100 ml water
¼ cup (generous) oz/50 g
 unsalted pistachios

Serves	4
Preparation time:	30 minutes
Cooking time:	35 minutes
Difficulty:	★ ★

Nougat was first created in Roman times by Apicius, the first gastronome to record his recipes in written form. Apicius made nougat out of honey, walnuts and eggs, but this original nougat recipe has evolved since ancient times. Today it forms the basis of Montelimar nougat, made with almonds; Provençal nougat made with coriander and anise; and finally, Antilles nougat, known as *pistache,* is made with peanuts.

Although still called nougat in Creole, the crisp pistachio mixture used for this dessert is actually nougatine. Crisp and delicious, nougatine is time-consuming but easy to prepare. Its rich amber color complements the green mousseline custard. For the best flavor and color, select bright green, unsalted pistachios for both the nougatine and the mousseline custard.

The nougatine may be prepared a day ahead and stored in the refrigerator until needed. Three disks of nougatine are needed for each serving. To make the disks, use a tart circle or design your own pattern with a piece of cardboard cut into a 4 inch/10 cm circle. Place the circle or pattern on the parchment paper and fill with the ground nougat. Remove the pattern before baking the nougatine rounds.

A wide range of flavors and ingredients may be substituted in this dessert. A few suggestions from our chef include: Almond nougatine with strawberry filling, hazelnut nougatine with raspberry filling—use your tastes and preferences to create your own variations.

1. For the pistachio mousseline, chop the pistachios finely and scrape the seeds from the vanilla bean. In a saucepan, bring the milk to a boil and steep the pistachios and vanilla bean in the hot liquid for 15 minutes. Whisk the yolks with the sugar and flour, then add the milk mixture. Return the cream to the saucepan and poach for 2 to 3 minutes until thick.

2. In a sauté pan, cook the sugar and water for about 10 minutes until they form a light caramel. Warm the pistachios in the oven and add them to the hot caramel. Pour the mixture onto a baking sheet to cool.

Pistachio Nougat

3. Once the nougatine is cold, crush it finely with a mortar and pestle. Place metal tart rings on a baking sheet lined with parchment paper. Fill the rings with the crushed nougatine, remove the rings and bake for 2 to 3 minutes. Cool and remove from the parchment paper.

4. While it is still warm, pour the pistachio cream into a bowl. Whisk in the softened butter and lime juice to make the mousseline, making sure no lumps of butter remain. Layer the nougatine circles and the pistachio mousseline on a plate and serve.

French Toast with

4 slices stale bread
3½ tbsp/50 g sugar
1 cup/250 ml whipping cream
2 eggs
6½ tbsp/100 ml white rum
1 cup/250 ml milk
1 stick liquorice
5¼ oz/150 g strawberries

For the preServes
2 cups/500 ml white rum
1 papaya
1 mangosteen
1 melon
1 kiwi
1 pineapple
1 mango
1 dragon fruit

Serves	4
Preparation time:	1 hour
Cooking time:	10 minutes
Cooling time:	1 month
Difficulty:	★ ★

We have given an original twist to the rustic flavor of French toast by pairing it with tropical fruit preserves. Like most old-fashioned recipes, it is a lesson in economy: The preserves can be made with whatever ripe fruit you may have in the refrigerator and the French toast is best when made with dry, stale bread, which absorbs the flavors of the custard better than fresh bread. If the bread you choose does not seem dry enough, toast it for a few minutes in the oven before soaking it in the custard.

Add your own personal touch to the French toast by flavoring the custard with vanilla or cinnamon instead of liquorice, or by using Triple Sec instead of rum. To fry the French toast, heat a few drops of oil with a tablespoon of butter. The oil will keep the milk solids in the butter from burning over high heat.

Burnt butter solids will leave black spots on the French toast slices and taste bitter.

The rum-covered fruit preserves that accompany this French toast are always good to have on hand. Not only do they keep well, but they improve with age, which is why we recommend preparing them at least one month in advance. Fill the jar to the rim and make sure all of the fruit is completely covered with the rum so that it will not turn brown or mold. These preserves also make an excellent topping for ice cream.

For a glistening red finish on the preserves, toss the fruit in a warm strawberry coulis made by cooking the strawberries with a little water. Serve the French toast with the warm fruit on a terra cotta plate to preserve this dessert's homespun charm.

1. To make the preserves, dice all of the fruit and place in a large jar. Cover the fruit with the rum and let marinate for at least one month in the refrigerator. Prepare a strawberry coulis by simmering the strawberries in a little water for 10 to 15 minutes. Stir the preserved fruit into the strawberry coulis.

2. Slice the stale bread into ½ in/1 cm thick slices and trim off the crusts.

Tropical Fruit Preserves

3. To make the rum-flavored custard for dipping the bread, mix the sugar with the whipping cream, then whisk in the eggs and the rum.

4. Heat the milk and steep the liquorice stick in it. Soak the slices of bread in the liquorice milk. Drain them, then dip in the rum custard. Brown the slices on each side in a frying pan with a little butter. Serve hot with the warm preserves on the side.

Florentine

4¼ oz/120 g crème fraîche
½ cup plus 2 tbsp/150 g sugar
2½ oz/50 g honey
2½ oz/50 g orange peel
2½ oz/75 g candied fruit
5¼ oz/150 g slivered almonds

For the chocolate coating:
3½ oz/100 g dark chocolate

Serves	4
Preparation time:	30 minutes
Cooking time:	25 minutes
Chilling time:	1 hour
Difficulty:	★

Weight-loss programs and nutritional fads aside, recent studies have shown that sugar, when consumed in moderation, is essential to a well-balanced diet. Sugar is absorbed rapidly into the digestive system, providing quick energy to muscles. To tempt the calorie-conscious, we have devised these bite-sized florentines. Small and deliciously sweet, they make an ideal accompaniment to afternoon tea.

The slivered almonds called for in this recipe keep the florentines flat and compact. Chopped walnuts or hazelnuts may be added to the florentine mixture but cannot be substituted for the almonds. Select a robust honey, such as

buckwheat or acacia flower, and add a hint of orange-flower water for a rich, complex flavor.

The look of these florentine palettes depends on the shapes and colors of the candied fruit chosen. We recommend brightly-colored fruits such as oranges, guavas and kumquats, which will show through the amber-colored batter.

To make evenly shaped, round florentines, you may use buttered tart rings to hold the batter in place while baking. Cool the florentines completely before dipping them in the tempered chocolate. Do not allow the chocolate to rise above a maximum temperature of 85 °F/30 °C for the chocolate coating.

1. In a saucepan over low heat, stir together the crème fraîche, sugar and honey.

2. Add the orange peel, candied fruit and slivered almonds and simmer for 5 to 6 minutes.

Palettes

3. Pour the batter onto a jelly-roll pan and bake at 350 °F/180 °C for 20 minutes until the florentine mixture turns a golden brown. Remove the pan with the florentine mixture from the oven. Allow the mixture to cool 1 minute before cutting it into circles with a round cutter. Cool the florentines completely.

4. Break the chocolate into small pieces and melt it in a double boiler. Dip each florentine into the tempered chocolate and place on a rack to drain off any excess chocolate. Chill 1 hour and serve decorated with bits of fresh and candied fruit.

Roasted Papayas

2 papayas
4 vanilla beans
1 can coconut milk
   (or ½ cup (generous)/50 g grated coconut
   and ¾ cup/200 ml coconut milk)
1 tbsp butter
8 tsp/40 g sugar

Serves	*4*
Preparation time:	*10 minutes*
Cooking time:	*50 minutes*
Difficulty:	*★*

The papaya is a large tropical fruit with a green and yellowish skin. Its soft, bright-orange flesh is refreshingly juicy and goes well with a splash of rum or lime juice. Unlike its cousin, the guava, the papaya has large, black inedible seeds which must be scraped out along with the thin membrane that encloses them.

For this dessert, select very ripe papayas. Slice the papayas in half and scrape out the seeds. Cut a small strip of the skin from the rounded side of the papaya half so that it will sit straight on the plate.

Roast the papayas in the serving dish to keep them from splitting or breaking when served. Our chef recommends combining fresh, grated coconut steeped in coconut milk for a more pronounced coconut flavor.

These roasted papayas offer a simple, satisfying end to any meal. Served warm, the papaya and coconut release their subtle flavors. A scoop of ice cream of your choice served alongside would round out the taste experience.

1. Split the papayas in half and scoop out the seeds without splitting or breaking the papaya flesh.

2. Cut the vanilla beans lengthwise, scrape the seeds into each papaya half, and lay the vanilla bean in the papaya.

with Coconut Milk

3. To make the coconut cream, heat the coconut milk and steep the freshly grated coconut in it for ½ hour.

4. Fill each papaya half with the coconut milk. Sprinkle the sides of the papaya with sugar and place on a greased baking sheet. Bake for 20 minutes at 450 °F/220 °C and serve warm.

Blanc-Mange with

2 egg whites
½ cup/125 g sugar
8 sheets of gelatin
8¾ oz/250 g fromage blanc
3½ oz/100 g cantaloupe

1 kiwi
2 cactus pears
2 passion fruit

1 cup/250 ml whipping cream

Serves	4
Preparation time:	30 minutes
Cooking time:	2 minutes
Chilling time:	1 hour
Difficulty:	★ ★

With its cloud-like look and texture, blanc mange is a dessert fit for the gods. Served with an ambrosia of tropical fruit, its subtle, melt-in-your-mouth flavor is pure paradise.

To cook the sugar syrup to soft-ball stage (250 °F/120 °C), you may use a candy thermometer or test the syrup with your fingers. To test the syrup, dip your fingers into a bowl of cold water then pull a small amount of the syrup out of the saucepan. Immediately dip your fingers into the cold water once more and test the consistency of the syrup. When the syrup can be shaped into a soft ball between your fingers, it is ready to be added to the meringue. Stir the softened gelatin sheets into the sugar syrup and pour the mixture over the egg whites.

Whisk the fromage blanc to aerate it before folding in the cooled meringue. Vanilla extract or ground cinnamon may be added to bring out its flavor. For a more exotic twist, add mango puree to the fromage blanc.

Chill the blanc mange in small ramekins and unmold them onto the serving plates. Garnish with a cascade of diced fruit and melon balls. Our chef has chosen to use the different colors of kiwis, cactus pears and cantaloupe but suggests you use your imagination to incorporate other colorful, flavorful fruits of your choice.

1. Using a mixer, beat the egg whites in a large bowl. Make a sugar syrup tby heating the sugar to the soft ball (250 °F/120 °C). Soften the gelatin sheets in cold water and add them to the sugar syrup.

2. Pour the syrup over the egg whites, beating continually until meringue is cool.

Tropical Fruit Cascade

3. Fold the meringue into the fromage blanc with a spatula, then spoon the mixture into small ramekins and refrigerate for 1 hour.

4. Scoop the cantaloupe into balls with a melon-baller and cut the kiwi and the cactus pear into small pieces. Unmold the blanc mange onto the plate and garnish it with a cascade of fruit. Dot the plate with passion fruit pulp and serve.

Fruit Kebabs

3 kiwis
1 papaya
½ dragon fruit
2 persimmons

7 oz/200 g litchis
4 oz/100 g red currants
1 cup/250 ml litchi liqueur
1 pomegranate

Serves	4
Preparation time:	30 minutes
Chilling time:	1 hour
Difficulty:	★

Alcohol and liqueurs are often added to pastries and desserts to heighten the flavor of the main ingredients. The litchi liqueur called for in this recipe is made by soaking litchis in a clear alcohol then distilling the resulting liquid. Sugar is then added to the liqueur before it undergoes the long aging and refining process. Only when the liqueur has reached the desired strength and maturity is it bottled and sold. Clear, strong and sweet, litchi liqueur goes perfectly with the tastes of the tropical fruit in this dessert. Passion fruit liqueur, orange liqueur or rum may also be used for a different flavor.

This easy, refreshing dessert requires a certain amount of time to assemble the fruit kebabs. Select firm-fleshed, brightly-colored fruit for a festival of colors on the plate. Dice all of the fruit and even out any cubes that seem larger than the others. Skewer the fruit with the toothpicks to make decorative, regular kebabs. Serve the fruit kebabs with a litchi cocktail for dipping. To make the litchi cocktail: Peel and chop the litchis and stir them into the litchi liqueur marinade.

This colorful, eye-catching dessert will brighten any cocktail tray, buffet table or dessert plate.

1. Cut the fruit into thin slices then dice into cubes ½ inch/1 cm on edge.

2. Macerate the fruits in the litchi liqueur, then drain the fruit and blend the liqueur with the litchis to make the dipping cocktail.

in Litchi Marinade

3. Skewer the fruit cubes onto toothpicks alternating colors.

4. Cut the pomegranate and remove the seeds. Insert the miniature fruit kebabs in the convex pomegranate half and refrigerate 1 hour. Blend the pomegranate seeds and add them to the litchi cocktail. Serve the fruit accompanied by the cocktail.

Bittersweet Chocolate

7 oz/200 g bittersweet chocolate
10 egg yolks
½ cup plus 2 tbsp/150 g sugar
1 quart/1 liter milk
¾ tsp/20 g unsweetened cocoa

Serves	*4*
Preparation time:	*20 minutes*
Cooking time:	*1 hour*
Chilling time:	*1 hour*
Difficulty:	★

Only the finest bittersweet chocolate should be used to make this simple but elegant dessert. Select a bittersweet chocolate with a high cocoa content (60 to 70 per cent) and melt it over low heat in a double boiler. For an even stronger flavor add a few drops of coffee extract to the melted chocolate.

It is best to prepare the mixture for steamed custards a day ahead, as for *pots de crème*, to prevent frothy egg bubbles from forming on the top when cooked.

Fill small, individual ramekins halfway full with the chocolate mixture, then set the ramekins in a pan filled with water, place the pan on the oven rack, and fill them to the rim with the rest of the mixture. This keeps the pots de crème from overflowing and dripping when they are placed in the oven.

This recipe may also be used to make one large chocolate terrine: Fill a terra-cotta loaf pan and steam it in a pan filled with water in the oven until set. Chill the terrine, unmold and decorate with warm chocolate sauce. Our chef also suggests trying this recipe with white chocolate. When using white chocolate reduce the amount of sugar called for in the recipe.

Refrigerate the pots de crème for at least one hour before serving. You may garnish the top with shaved white or dark chocolate or sprinkle them with unsweetened cocoa.

1. Break or chop the chocolate into small pieces and melt it in a double boiler, stirring occasionally.

2. Whisk the egg yolks with the sugar until they turn pale yellow in color.

Pots de Crème

3. In a saucepan, bring the milk to a boil and add to the melted chocolate and stir with a wooden spoon for 2 minutes.

4. Whisk the chocolate and milk mixture into the egg mixture. Fill individual ramekins to the rim with the chocolate cream. Place the pots de crème in a pan filled with water in the oven and steam for 1 hour at 212 °C/100 °F. Cool and refrigerate at least 1 hour before serving. Sprinkle with cocoa powder.

Poached Pears with Tropical

4 pears
3 cups/750 ml sugar syrup (see
   basic recipe)
2 tbsp/20 g unsalted pistachios, chopped

For the champagne sorbet:
2 cups/500 ml champagne

For the tropical spice sauce:
8-10 whole cloves
1 star anise
1 stick liquorice
1 whole nutmeg

Serves	4
Preparation time:	20 minutes
Cooking time:	25 minutes
Freezing time:	1 hour
Difficulty:	★ ★

Because this recipe requires poaching the pears, select firm fruit which resist heat well. Williams or Comice pears work well for poaching. Their skin should be firm, green and unblemished. Should you choose to modify the recipe and poach other fruits such as peaches or guavas, use the same criteria for selection.

The cloves add heat and spice to the poaching liquid, which is also flavored with star anise and liquorice. Once poached, the pears take on the subtle flavors of all the spices for a complex tasting experience.

Poaching involves cooking peeled fruit in a simmering liquid over low heat. The pears in this recipe should be dropped into hot, but not boiling, sugar syrup in order to retain all their

sugar and flavor. The hot sugar syrup will seize the fruit so that it retains its shape. The strained poaching liquid is used to make both the champagne sorbet and the spice sauce for this dessert. For the sauce, add a teaspoon of cornstarch diluted in a small amount of water to one cup of the hot syrup, then cool. The resulting sauce will be rich amber in color, shiny and smooth.

We have cut the poached pears in half and filled them with champagne sorbet in our presentation of this dessert. You may also serve the pears whole with a scoop of refreshing champagne sorbet on the side. Accompany this dessert with a glass of dry champagne or a good sparkling wine for a festive touch to the end of a meal.

1. Peel and core the pears. If you are not poaching the pears immediately, rub them with lemon juice to keep them from turning brown.

2. In a saucepan, heat the sugar syrup with the spices over low heat. Simmer for 10 minutes then drop the pears in. Poach the pears for 15 minutes, turning them from time to time to insure they cook evenly. Drain the pears and chill.

Spices and Champagne Sorbet

3. To make the champagne sorbet, strain the syrup used in poaching and pour 2 cups/500 ml into a bowl. Set aside the spices used in the poaching syrup for decoration. Whisk the champagne into the liquid, then turn the sorbet in an ice cream machine until firm and freeze for 1 hour.

4. Cut each pear in half. Stick the cloves used in the poaching syrup around the top of each pear. Place the bottom half of the pear in a round mold or tart ring. Spread a thick layer of sorbet on the pear and cover with the top of the pear. Drizzle the remaining 1 cup/250 ml of syrup over the pears, sprinkle with chopped pistachios and serve.

Caramelized Apples with

4 apples
3½ tbsp/50 g butter
3½ tbsp/50 g brown sugar
¾ cup/200 ml dark rum

For the ice cream:
3 cups/750 ml milk
1 cinnamon stick

1 cup/250 ml unsweetened
   condensed milk
12 egg yolks
1 cup/250 g sugar
3½ tbsp/100 g crème fraîche
⅓ cup/50 g black raisins
⅓ cup/50 g golden raisins

Serves   4
Preparation time: 30 minutes
Cooking time: 25 minutes
Chilling time: 1 hour
Difficulty: ★

Is the apple truly the oldest fruit, and can we really reproach Adam and Eve for having been unable to resist the sweet temptation to bite into one? All over the world, wild and domestic apple trees flower and produce in abundance. Apples were a favorite fruit of the Greeks and Romans; the Gauls were among the first to make apple cider. The countless apple varieties created over the centuries are just as sought after today as they were in the past.

We have chosen to use sweet apples such as Golden Delicious or Starking instead of cooking apples for this recipe. These apple varieties, which originated in America and

Australia, can be found year-round, though they are at their best in the autumn and winter, between October and April. Select firm, ripe unblemished fruit which will hold its shape when caramelized and a high-quality butter. The brown sugar used to make the caramel adds rustic flavor to the apples.

Rum-raisin ice cream is a Caribbean dessert classic. Here it is made with two types of raisins and crème fraîche for a smooth, creamy, flavorful result. Just before serving, flambée the apples with warmed dark or white rum to bring out the contrast between the warm apples and the cold ice cream.

1. Macerate the raisins in the rum overnight and peel and core the apples. Cut each apple in half and each half into 5 slices.

2. To make the ice cream, bring the milk to a boil in a saucepan and steep the cinnamon in it. Add the condensed milk to the mixture. Whisk together the egg yolks and the sugar, bring the milk mixture back to a boil and pour it over the yolks and sugar, stirring constantly. Add the crème fraîche and the raisins and cool before turning in an ice cream maker.

Rum-Raisin Ice Cream

3. In a large frying pan, melt the butter and sugar until the sugar caramelizes to a light brown. Brown the apples in the caramel, turning once or twice to cook evenly, and drain on an aluminum baking sheet.

4. Turn the ice cream in an ice cream maker and place in the freezer for 1 hour. Fan the warm apple slices out in a circle on the plate, place a scoop of ice cream in the center of the apple crown and serve, garnished with a sprig of mint.

Orange Profiteroles with

For the choux pastry:
1 cup/250 ml milk
6½ tbsp/100 g butter
a pinch of salt
4 eggs
2 egg yolks

For the ice cream:
zest and juice of 2 oranges
2 cups/500 ml crème anglaise (see
   basic recipe)
1 tbsp crème fraîche

For the caramelized star fruit:
4 tsp/20 g brown sugar
4 tsp/20 g butter
1 star fruit

For the chocolate sauce:
2 oz/60 g bittersweet chocolate
2½ tbsp/40 ml sugar syrup (see
   basic recipe)

Serves   4
Preparation time: 30 minutes
Cooking time: 1 hour 30 minutes
Difficulty: ★

These little cream puffs filled with orange ice cream sit on star-shaped beds of mildly caramelized star fruit.

To make the orange ice cream, bring the orange juice and pulp to a boil. Stir in the crème anglaise and allow to cool completely, then turn the ice cream in an ice cream maker. Our chef recommends adding the crème fraîche to the ice cream while still soft in the ice cream maker for an extra creamy texture. This ice cream recipe may also be made with other citrus fruits.

Scoop the ice cream into small balls ahead of time and store in the freezer until you are ready to serve the profiteroles.

Lightly caramelize the star fruit slices with the butter and brown sugar. Arrange the fruit slices around one side of the plate. Coat each profiterole with the chocolate sauce and set on top of the star fruit. Garnish the plate with chocolate sauce, julienned candied orange and toasted slivered almonds, if desired.

1. In a saucepan, bring the milk, butter and salt to a boil. Remove the pan from the heat and stir the flour into the boiling liquid with a wooden spoon. Dry the dough out by heating it over low heat for 15 minutes, stirring constantly.

2. Add the eggs one by one to the dough, stirring vigorously. Make the orange ice cream mixture and turn it in an ice cream machine until smooth and creamy. For the chocolate sauce, melt the chocolate in a double-boiler with the sugar syrup.

Caramelized Star Fruit

3. Using a pastry bag fitted with a round tip, pipe the cream puffs onto a baking sheet lined with parchment paper. Brush the cream puffs with the egg yolks and score with the back of a fork. Bake at 375 °F/190 °C for 30 minutes until brown and dry. While the cream puffs are baking, caramelize the star fruit with the brown sugar and butter in a frying pan.

4. To assemble the dessert, place slices of caramelized star fruit on each plate. Halve the cream puffs and set the bottoms on the star fruit slices. Scoop the orange ice cream onto each cream puff. Dip the tops in the chocolate sauce and set on the ice cream. Serve immediately.

Sweet Potato Ravioli

1 package ravioli squares
1 egg yolk

For the sweet potato filling:
2 sweet potatoes
3½ tbsp/50 g sugar
1 oz/30 g ground cinnamon
a pinch of allspice
8 tsp/40 g butter
1 egg yolk

For the cinnamon sauce:
¾ cup/200 ml heavy cream
juice of 1 orange
2 cinnamon sticks
3½ tbsp/50 g sugar

Serves	4
Preparation time:	30 minutes
Cooking time:	2 hours
Difficulty:	★ ★

Indigenous to South America, the sweet potato has a dark pink skin and mauve flesh. Nearly 100 varieties of sweet potato can be found in the Caribbean Isles, many of them growing wild. Our chef has chosen a sweet potato variety which is cultivated especially for use in desserts.

The term, "ravioli" comes from the Genoan word *rabioles* meaning "little pieces." It is believed that ravioli were first invented to make use of the small bits of leftover pasta dough. Today, Italian ravioli are small pockets of pasta dough which surround a pre-cooked filling.

For this recipe, prepare at least four ravioli per person. For a lovely round shape, cut the ravioli with a fluted cutter before cooking them in boiling water. The ravioli are done when they rise to the surface of the water. Remove the ravioli and drain them on a clean dishtowel before placing them on the plate.

The cinnamon sauce called for in this dessert will highlight the cinnamon flavor in the ravioli filling. Bring the heavy cream and the orange juice to a boil and steep the cinnamon sticks in the sauce. Coat the ravioli with the sauce just before serving.

Quick and simple, this recipe may also be made with a cooked apple filling rather than sweet potatoes. To tempt gourmet guests even further, sprinkle chopped nuts such as almonds, hazelnuts or pistachios over the cinnamon sauce.

1. Cut the sweet potatoes in half and sprinkle each half with sugar. Tightly wrap the halves individually in aluminum foil and bake for 1½ hours at 400 °F/200 °C. Once the potatoes are done, scrape out the insides and mash together with the cinnamon, allspice and the egg yolk, blending all ingredients well.

2. Brush the edges of the ravioli with the egg yolk. Spoon a small amount of the sweet potato filling into the center of each ravioli square.

with Cinnamon Sauce

3. Place a second ravioli square on top of the filling. Working from the center, seal the ravioli with the sides of your hands to eliminate any air around the filling, then cut with a fluted cutter. Bring a pot of water to a boil. Drop the ravioli one by one into the boiling water and cook for 1 to 2 minutes or until the ravioli rise to the surface. Drain well.

4. To make the cinnamon sauce, bring the orange juice and the heavy cream to a boil in a sauce pan and steep the cinnamon sticks in the mixture. Stir in the sugar. Place the hot ravioli on the plate and cover them well with the warm sauce. Serve immediately.

Vanilla Ravioli

For the crêpe batter:
1 cup/125 g flour
¼ cup/55 g sugar
a pinch of salt
4 eggs
2 cups/500 ml milk
1 tbsp/15 g butter

For the tamarind sauce:
1 oz/30 g tamarind
1 cup/250 ml tamarind juice

For the chiboust cream:
2½ tbsp/40 ml heavy cream
3 eggs, separated
4 tsp/20 g sugar
¾ oz/20 g instant custard mix
1 sheet of gelatin
3 vanilla beans

Serves	*4*
Preparation time:	*1 hour*
Cooking time:	*15 minutes*
Resting time:	*2 hours*
Difficulty:	★ ★

The distinctive flavors of vanilla and tamarind brought together in the chiboust cream and the sauce are what makes this dessert unique.

This recipe calls for a classic crêpe batter. If you prepare the crêpes in a skillet or frying pan, you will need to cut out small circles from the crêpes to make the ravioli. Instead, we recommend preparing small, individual crêpes in a blini pan. This saves time by eliminating the need to cut the crêpes into smaller rounds and avoids wasting the resulting leftover bits of crêpe. For light, even crêpes, prepare the batter well ahead of time so that it has a chance to rest for at least two hours.

Chiboust cream is named for the Parisian pastry chef who invented the famous Saint Honore pastry in the 19th century. For a chiboust cream which is smooth and airy, carefully incorporate the beaten egg whites into the warm custard. Refrigerate the cream for a half hour until firm enough to pipe or spoon into the ravioli. Other flavor possibilities for the chiboust cream include cinnamon, citrus zest or orange juice.

Once you have made the small crêpe rounds, fold them in half over the chiboust cream, adhering the edges to the cream well so that they do not come open or dry out when baked. Bake the ravioli directly in the serving dishes you plan to use.

1. For the crêpe batter, stir together the dry ingredients then whisk in the eggs. Add the milk little by little, whisking constantly to obtain a smooth batter. Refrigerate the batter for 2 hours. Melt the butter in a frying pan and sauté the crêpes, flipping them once to brown them on both sides.

2. Cut each of the crêpes into circles using a 3 inch/8 cm cutter. To make the tamarind sauce, blend the tamarinds with the tamarind juice.

with Tamarind Sauce

3. To make the chiboust cream, whisk together the egg yolks, sugar and instant custard mix. Bring the milk to a boil with the scraped vanilla bean. Pour the milk over the egg mixture, return the custard to the saucepan and cook for 2 to 3 minutes over low heat. Soften the gelatin sheet in cold water and add it to the custard. Beat the egg whites to stiff peaks. Fold the whites into the custard and chill.

4. Fill the crêpe rounds with the chiboust cream using a pastry bag fitted with a round tip. Fold the crêpes in half, place on an oven-proof plate or serving dish and bake for 3 minutes at 350 °F/180 °C. Garnish the plate with tamarind sauce and serve hot.

For the rice pudding
1½ cups/250 g short-grain rice
5 cups/1250 ml milk
1 vanilla bean
⅓ cup/80 g sugar
1 tbsp crème fraîche
1 egg yolk

2 mangosteens
1 mango
1 pineapple
2 pomegranates
1 candied angelica stick
4 candied cherries
3½ oz/100 g dark chocolate

Serves	*4*
Preparation time:	*30 minutes*
Cooking time:	*35 minutes*
Resting time:	*10 minutes*
Difficulty:	★

Rice is the most commonly cultivated grain in tropical, equatorial and temperate zones. Many varieties exist: long-grain, short-grain, high-gluten or sticky rice, just to name a few. Our chef recommends using a high-quality, round, short-grain rice such as the Italian Arborio variety used for risotto. Short-grain rice contains more starch and will not fall apart after extended cooking. Blanching the rice before boiling it in the vanilla milk will eliminate some of the starch from the rice and keep the pudding from becoming too thick and sticky.

When making Tahitian rice pudding, it is important to steep the halved and scraped vanilla bean well in the milk. Infuse the milk with the vanilla as long as possible so that it absorbs a maximum of vanilla flavor. You may accentuate the flavor of the milk even further by adding the zest of an orange as well. Crème fraîche and an egg yolk are added at the end of the cooking time to set the pudding and give it a creamy texture.

To plate the dessert: Shape quenelles of rice pudding with two soup spoons, rolling the pudding from one spoon to the other to obtain an even, three-sided oval shape. The rice pudding may also be spooned into molds of your choice and set. Serve the rice pudding warm or cold garnished with small drops of chocolate to decorate the plate.

1. Place the rice in a saucepan and cover with cold water. Blanch it over low heat for 2 to 3 minutes. In another saucepan, bring the milk to a boil with the vanilla bean. Drain the water from the rice and pour the rice directly into the boiling milk.

2. Peel and slice the fruit. Break the dark chocolate into small pieces and melt in a double boiler.

Rice Pudding

3. Cook the rice in the milk for 15 minutes or until it is soft and most of the milk has been absorbed. Remove the vanilla bean and reserve for decoration. Stir in the sugar, crème fraîche and egg yolk, and refrigerate until cool.

4. Shape quenelles out of the chilled rice pudding. Place 3 quenelles on each plate. Arrange the fruit in a decorative pattern around the quenelles. Garnish the plate with the melted chocolate and strips of vanilla bean.

Candied Victoria

For the shortbread:
1⅔ cup/200 g flour
⅓ cup/50 g confectioners' sugar
a pinch of baking powder
zest of 1 lemon
10 tbsp/150 g butter
1 egg

For the pastry cream:
1 cup/250 ml milk
1 vanilla bean

3 egg yolks
3½ tbsp/50 g sugar
¼ cup/30 g flour

1 Victoria pineapple
6½ tbsp/150 g glucose or corn syrup
¼ cup/60 g brown sugar
3½ oz/100 g chocolate

Serves	*4*
Preparation time:	*40 minutes*
Cooking time:	*20 minutes*
Resting time:	*2 hours*
Difficulty:	*★*

The pineapple is a tropical plant whose large fruit develops from a profusion of flowers. In English, the pineapple gets its name from its resemblance to a pine cone. The scientific name for pineapple, *Ananas comosus*, comes from the Guarani word *ana-ana* which means "flavor of flavors." Available year-round, pineapples contain an enzyme which absorbs fat and aids digestion, making it an ideal dessert fruit. Our chef recommends the small, round, sweet Victoria pineapple for this recipe.

The shortbread should be prepared ahead of time: Our chef recommends a full day before The lemon in the dough complements the tart flavor of the candied pineapple topping. Use your fingers to rub the ingredients of the dough together. Knead the dough lightly into a ball and refrigerate.

To candy the pineapple, heat the glucose with the brown sugar, place the pineapple slices in the syrup and cook over low heat for three minutes. Cover the pan with plastic wrap and let cool: The pineapple will absorb the sugar yet retain its golden color. Drain the pineapple slices well before assembling the dessert to keep the shortbread from getting soggy.

Roll out the shortbread dough and cut circles the size of the pineapple slices. Bake on a baking sheet lined with parchment paper. Once the shortbread has cooled, thin the pastry cream with a small amount of lemon juice or frangipane (see basic recipe) and spread the pastry cream over the shortbread. Place the pineapple slice on top. Fill the hole in the center of the pineapple slice with the melted chocolate or whipped cream.

1. For the shortbread, stir together the flour, confectioners' sugar, baking powder and lemon zest. Rub the butter into the dry ingredients with your fingers. Make a well in the center of the mixture, break the egg in the center of the well and stir it into the mixture with your fingers, incorporating the flour bit by bit. Knead the dough lightly 2 or 3 times to shape a round ball of dough. Refrigerate 2 to 3 hours.

2. Peel the pineapple and cut it into round slices. Remove the core. Roll out the shortbread dough and cut it into circles with a 4 in/10 cm cutter. Bake the shortbread for 10 minutes at 350 °F/180 °C or until it begins to turn light brown around the edges.

Pineapple Tart

3. Bring the glucose to a boil with the brown sugar. Drop the pineapple slices in the liquid and cook for 3 minutes. Cover the saucepan with plastic wrap and let cool. Drain the slices on a clean dishtowel. Prepare the pastry cream.

4. To assemble the dessert, spread the pastry cream onto each shortbread round. Place a slice of candied pineapple on top and fill the center of the pineapple slices with melted chocolate.

Fruit Salad with

1 pineapple
1 papaya
1 kiwi
1 grapefruit
14 oz/400 g litchis
1 vanilla bean
3½ tbsp/50 ml white rum

For the sabayon cream:
8 egg yolks
⅔ cup/150 ml sugar syrup (see basic recipe)
2 cups/500 ml whipping cream

For the garnish:
mint leaves
pomegranate seeds
grated coconut

Serves	*4*
Preparation time:	*30 minutes*
Cooking time:	*10 minutes*
Chilling time:	*1 hour*
Difficulty:	*★*

Italian in origin, the sabayon mousse calls for a large number of egg yolks which are high in protein, lipids and vitamins. It is made by whisking egg yolks with sugar syrup over low heat until a frothy, yellow mousse forms. After the mousse has cooled, whipped cream is folded into it.

When whisking the egg and syrup mixture for the sabayon, place your hand on the side of the saucepan to insure the mixture does not get too hot. This will keep the sabayon from overcooking and sticking to the bottom of the pot. Beat the mixture vigorously for ten minutes over the heat until thick and creamy, using an electric mixer, if desired. Cool the egg mixture completely before incorporating the whipped cream.

Dice the fruit and macerate it in the rum to enhance the flavor. Spoon the fruit into parfait glasses and top with the sabayon. Roast the coconut in the oven to add flavor and crispness. For color and decoration, dot the sabayon with the pomegranate seeds and sprinkle with the roasted coconut.

This fruit salad may be made with other fruits of your choice. Champagne, Grand Marnier or other alcohols may be used to macerate the fruit as well.

1. Carefully peel the fruit. Split and scrape the vanilla bean. Dice all fruit and macerate it with the rum and the vanilla bean.

2. To make the sabayon, beat the egg yolks lightly in a sauce pan. Add the sugar syrup and cook over low heat, whisking constantly, for about 10 minutes until the mixture is thick and frothy, then place in the refrigerator for 1 hour.

Soufflé

3. In a bowl, whisk the egg yolks with the sugar and instant custard powder. Pour the boiling coconut milk over the egg mixture, stirring constantly, and return the custard to the saucepan. Cook over low heat for 5 to 7 minutes until thick. Cool completely, then beat the egg whites to stiff peaks and fold them into the cooled pastry cream.

4. Spoon the soufflé mixture into the coconut shells, then place each shell on a rounded base to hold it upright. Run your fingertip around the edge of the soufflé to detach it from the sides of the coconut and enable it to rise evenly. Bake for 15 minutes at 450 °F/250 °C and serve immediately, sprinkled with grated coconut.

Spiced Clementine-

1 grapefruit
4 clementines
1 cup/250 ml milk
3 peppercorns
1 whole clove
1 star anise
½ tsp ground cinnamon
3 egg yolks
½ cup plus 1 tbsp/130 g sugar
6 egg whites

For the roux:
3½ tbsp/50 g butter
½ cup/60 g flour

For the garnish:
1 tsp cinnamon
4 tsp confectioners' sugar

Serves	4
Preparation time:	30 minutes
Cooking time:	30 minutes
Difficulty:	★ ★

Our chef has created this recipe to combine the flavors of two citrus fruits: clementines and grapefruit. Triple Sec or other citrus liqueurs may be used to further enhance the tart, slightly bitter taste of the fruit. To improve flavor and texture, diced candied grapefruit, citron, orange or clementine may also be added to the soufflé. The spices we suggest here—clove, pepper, star anise and cinnamon—have been specially selected to bring out the flavor of the fruit, although vanilla, cardamom and allspice also work quite well.

For best results, our chef recommends folding the beaten egg whites into the sweet bèchamel base while the sauce is still warm. When filling the soufflé molds, use a metal spatula to smooth the tops, then run the tip of your finger around the edge of each soufflé to detach it from the sides of the mold. The resulting soufflés will then rise straight and cook evenly.

Just before serving, sprinkle the tops of the soufflés with the ground cinnamon and confectioners' sugar, adn serve straight from the oven, before the soufflés have time to fall. Your breathtakingly light citrus soufflés will be a sure sign to your guests that you have mastered the soufflé technique.

1. Squeeze the juice of the grapefruit and 2 of the clementines into a saucepan. Peel and segment the other 2 clementines. Add the milk and spices to the juice and bring to a boil.

2. To prepare the roux, melt the butter in a saucepan, stir in the flour and cook the roux until it is frothy and white, stirring constantly with a wooden spoon.

Grapefruit Soufflé

3. Strain the milk and juice mixture into the roux. In a separate bowl, whisk the yolks with 6½ tbsp/100 g of the sugar, then beat them into the juice and milk mixture. Cook over low heat, while beating, for several minutes to obtain a sweet bèchamel sauce.

4. Beat the egg whites with the rest of the sugar until they form stiff peaks, then fold the meringue into the sweet bèchamel sauce. Line the bottom of the soufflé molds with clementine segments, fill the molds to the rim with the soufflé mixture, and bake in a hot oven for 15 minutes. Sprinkle with cinnamon and confectioners' sugar and serve immediately.

For the vanilla pastry cream:
3 vanilla beans
2 cups/500 ml milk
6 egg yolks
6½ tbsp/100 g sugar
½ cup plus 1 tbsp flour

For the meringue:
6 egg whites
3½ tbsp/50 g sugar

To line the soufflé molds:
1 tbsp butter, softened
2 tbsp sugar

For the garnish:
2 tbsp confectioners' sugar

Serves 4
Preparation time: 30 minutes
Cooking time: 15 minutes
Difficulty: ★ ★

Smooth and light as a cloud, this dessert soufflé with the incomparable flavor of vanilla will make a stunning end to any meal. Carefully butter and sugar the molds to prevent the soufflé from sticking to the sides while baking. Brush the bottom and the sides of the mold with softened butter, then dust with sugar to coat the mold completely.

Carefully fold the meringue into the pastry cream with a spatula using a circular motion from bottom to top. Spoon the mixture into individual molds or one large soufflé dish. Chef's hint: One trick which will help the soufflé rise evenly is to run your finger around the edge of each soufflé to detach the soufflé mixture from the mold.

Place the soufflés in the microwave for two minutes before baking in a hot oven for five to six minutes. Do not open the oven during this time, even out of curiosity. The change in temperature cause by even cracking the door may well cause the soufflé to fall.

When the soufflés are done, remove them from the oven and sprinkle with confectioners' sugar. Bring them to the table immediately before the soufflés have a chance to fall.

1. Butter and sugar the molds with the softened butter and a pinch of sugar. Tap out any excess sugar.

2. To make the vanilla pastry cream, split and scrape the vanilla beans, place them in the milk, and bring the milk to a boil. Whisk the egg yolks together with the sugar and flour. Remove the vanilla beans from the milk and pour the hot milk over the egg yolks, whisking constantly. Heat the pastry cream for 2 to 3 minutes over low heat until thick.

Vanilla Soufflé

3. To make the meringue, beat the egg whites with the sugar until they form stiff peaks.

4. Gently fold the meringue into the warm pastry cream. Fill the soufflé molds to the rim and detach the mixture from the edges of the molds. Bake for 12 to 13 minutes at 425 °F/220 °C, sprinkle with confectioners' sugar and serve hot.

Soursop Soup

1 soursop
¾ cup plus 1 tbsp/200 g sugar
6½ tbsp curaçao
1 cup/250 ml water
10½ oz/300 g kumquats
½ pint red currants

Serves	*4*
Preparation time:	*10 minutes*
Cooking time:	*3 minutes*
Chilling time:	*30 minutes*
Difficulty:	*★*

Curaçao is an orange liqueur originally distilled by the Dutch who colonized the Caribbean island of the same name. Made with the peel of citrus fruits, the liqueur is popular today in cocktails and as an after dinner drink. Of the various colors of Curaçao on the market—clear, blue, green and pink—blue Curaçao is by far the most well-known.

The sour and bitter flavor of the kumquats goes well with the mild, sweet taste of the soursop in this cold soup. The firm skin of the soursop makes a perfect bowl, but the creamy, white flesh of the soursop is full of inedible hard, black seeds which must be removed before eating. To save time, our chef recommends chopping the soursop flesh along with the seeds in a blender or food processor set at a low speed. Strain the resulting pulp through a fine sieve to remove the seeds.

For a tarter citrus flavor, chopped lime may be substituted for the kumquats. Make sure to taste the soup before serving to test the flavor. Water may be added if the soup is too sweet.

Simple and easy to prepare, this dessert can be whipped up at the last minute and served chilled to friends lounging around the pool on a hot summer day.

1. Select a ripe, black-spined soursop which does not have too many black spots on its skin. Cut a slice from the side, leaving ¾ of the fruit intact to serve as a soup bowl.

2. Using a sharp knife, scoop out the center of the soursop without breaking the skin.

with Blue Curaçao

3. In a saucepan, bring the sugar and water to a boil, and cook for 3 minutes to make a sugar syrup. Blend the soursop flesh in a food processor or blender at low speed, strain the pulp to remove the seeds, then add the sugar syrup and the curaçao.

4. Chop the kumquats into small pieces, reserving 3 or 4 for the garnish. Add the diced kumquat to the soup. Fill the soursop shell with the soup and garnish with kumquat slices and red currants. Refrigerate 30 minutes before serving.

Tropical Fruit Soup

1 grapefruit
1 mangosteen
1 pineapple
1 mango
1 kiwi
7 oz/200 g litchis
1 papaya
1 banana

For the juice:
1¼ cups/300 ml sugar syrup (see basic recipe)
¾ cup/200 ml passion fruit liqueur
1 vanilla bean, split and scraped
pinch of pepper

For the garnish:
8 mint leaves
2 passion fruit

Serves	*4*
Preparation time:	*25 minutes*
Cooking time:	*10 minutes*
Chilling time:	*1 hour*
Difficulty:	★

This recipe is simplicity in itself. Our chef has selected a wide range of exotic fruits for this tropical soup, but feel free to improvise on his choices and use your imagination when selecting the fruit. While other fruit substitutions work just as well, we recommend using passion fruit as we have here as it lends a slightly sour flavor to this dessert.

Slice the fruit on a cutting board with a grooved-edge to catch all of the juice. Reserve the juice and add it to the soup. When slicing the fruit, remember to pit the mangosteens and cut out the eyes of the pineapple. Chop the mint finely with a sharp knife to keep it from turning black.

To assemble the dessert: Arrange the fruit in a small bowl or dish, alternating shapes and colors. Pour the juice over the fresh fruit and garnish with mint and passion fruit seeds. The pale orange pulp of the passion fruit adds color and flavor.

Refreshing and easy to prepare, this recipe makes an ideal last-minute dessert. Serve it chilled after a heavy meal.

1. Peel all the fruit and segment the grapefruit and the mangosteen. Cut the other fruit into small pieces, reserving any juice for the soup.

2. Finely chop the mint leaves with a sharp knife.

with Fresh Mint

3. To make the soup, prepare the syrup by boiling equal amounts of water and sugar. Stir in the reserved fruit juice and the passion fruit liqueur. Add the split and scraped vanilla bean and the pepper and refrigerate for at least 1 hour.

4. To assemble the dessert, arrange the fruit in a bowl or dish. Pour the soup slowly over it, garnish with the mint and passion fruit, and serve chilled.

Pink Grapefruit

4 grapefruit
14 oz/400 g dried fruit: pecans, hazelnuts,
  pistachios, peanuts, almonds, raisins
½ cup plus 2 tbsp/150 g sugar
⅔ cup/150 ml water
4 egg whites

Serves	*4*
Preparation time:	*15 minutes*
Cooking time:	*5 minutes*
Difficulty:	*★*

Grapefruit are large citrus fruits with yellow or greenish-yellow skin. Native to Asia, grapefruit have a tart, acidic pulp. They can be candied, squeezed into juice, or made into jam. Pink grapefruit, a hybrid variety produced by crossing a grapefruit with an orange, have been selected for this desert because they tend to be sweeter than yellow grapefruit, but lower in sugar than oranges. Another option is the pomelo or Chinese grapefruit, known as "the forbidden fruit" in the French Antilles.

To prepare a pomelo, make several sharp incisions in the skin and peel it away entirely, along with the pith surrounding the segments. Both skin and pith are too bitter to eat raw, and must be candied before they become palatable. One serving suggestion is to alternate grapefruit and pomelos in the four servings of this Pink Grapefruit Surprise.

The list of dried fruit and nuts given in the ingredients can be augmented or altered, depending on taste and availability. As an added touch, you may want to spoon a bit of orange, guava or lemon marmalade into the bottom of the grapefruit before filling it and topping with the meringue.

1. Using a sharp knife with a thin blade, serrate the tops of the grapefruit and remove these lids.

2. Scrape the pulp from the grapefruit shell, removing all membranes and pith. Chop the segments and drain in a strainer.

Surprise

3. To make the filling, chop the dried fruit coarsely and toss together with the grapefruit pieces. Fill each grapefruit with this mixture.

4. For the syrup, bring the sugar and water to a boil and cook to the soft ball stage (250 °F/120 °C). Beat the egg whites to stiff peaks, pour the sugar syrup over them, and beat continuously until cooled. Pipe the meringue onto the top of each grapefruit with a pastry bag. Place the grapefruit under the broiler for 3–4 minutes until they begin to brown and serve immediately.

Cardamom-Mango

14 oz/400 g puff pastry (see
 basic recipe)
2 mangos
a pinch of cardamom

For the frangipane:
3½ tbsp/50 g butter
4 tsp/20 g sugar
1 egg yolk
½ cup/60 g almond flour

For the mango coulis:
6½ tbsp/100 ml mango pulp
2 cups/500 ml sugar syrup (see
 basic recipe)

Serves   4
Preparation time: 1 hour
Cooking time: 1 hour 5 minutes
Difficulty: ★

Cardamom is an aromatic plant originally growing on the island of Malabar. It produces a fruit with a green pod containing fragrant black seeds which are ground and used as a spice after the pods have dried.

Cardamom is a common ingredient in Middle Eastern and Asian cooking and is often used to flavor coffee. Our chef has chosen to combine the peppery flavor of cardamom with the sweet, tropical taste of mango for an especially delicate balance of flavors. Prepare the puff pastry dough according to the basic recipe or you may use store-bought puff pastry. Roll the dough out to a thickness of ¹⁄₁₆ inch/2-3 mm, and refrigerate the rolled dough for 10 to 15 minutes.

To make the tarts: Cut the puff pastry into the desired shape with a pastry cutter and prick it with a fork to prevent it from puffing up while baking. Be sure to check the consistency of the frangipane before spreading it over the the pastry: If it is either too thick or too thin, it can damage the pastry shell and cause it to leak. Fan the mango slices out onto the frangipane. Using a pepper grinder, sprinkle fresh or crushed cardamom over the mango, and bake in a hot oven.

Serve the tarts with a mango or papaya coulis made by blending the fruit pulp with the sugar syrup. These tarts may also be made with other tropical fruits like guava or papaya and served with a scoop of exotic fruit sorbet.

1. Roll out the puff pastry to a thickness of ¹⁄₁₆ in/2-3 mm. Use a pastry cutter to cut out fluted ovals, prick each with a fork and refrigerate.

2. Peel the mangos and slice the 2 lobes of each mango from the core. Slice the fruit thinly and roast the slices, covered with 1 tbsp butter, ¼ tsp sugar and a pinch of cardamom, for 15 minutes at 375-400 °F/180-200 °C. Allow to cool.

Tart

3. To make the fruit coulis, blend together the mango pulp and the sugar syrup. To make the frangipane, soften the butter. Add the sugar, egg yolk and almond flour and mix well.

4. Spread the puff pastry ovals with the frangipane. Carefully arrange slices of roasted mango on the puff pastry and bake for 15 minutes at 350 °F/180 °C. Place each mango tart on a plate and garnish with the mango coulis.

Ti Moune Fromage

1 cup/250 g sweet pastry(see
   basic recipes)
3 eggs, separated
½ cup/125 g sugar
3½ tbsp/50 g butter, melted

10½ oz/300 g fromage blanc
¼ cup/30 g flour
½ cup plus 1 tbsp/75 g raisins
½ jar guava jam

Serves   4
Preparation time: 30 minutes
Cooking time: 30 minutes
Difficulty: ★

Cheese production dates back to the very first livestock breeders. To make use of the surplus of milk which would not keep, the breeders would let the milk curdle then beat the curds with thick branches until smooth. They then pressed the resulting paste under stones to remove the whey and make what we now call fresh cheese. This process was an excellent means of conserving milk which otherwise needed to be consumed immediately. Cheese, served with bread, even appears several times in the Bible as a symbol of welcome and hospitality.

For this tart, the chef recommends using fromage blanc, or for fewer calories, a whole-milk yogurt, both of which are tarter and lighter than cream or crème fraîche. The raisins called for

in the recipe may be plumped in ¼ cup of alcohol of your choice for added flavor, if you wish.

Cut out circles of sweet dough slightly larger than the tart forms to be used. Lightly press the dough into the forms, cover with parchment paper, and fill with beans or rice to weigh down the dough and hold it in place during the pre-baking.

Once in the oven, the fromage blanc filling of the cheesecake will puff up like a soufflé. This dessert must be served hot from the oven to maintain this soufflé aspect. Guests and children alike will enjoy this cheesecake as a snack or dessert.

1. Press the sweet pastry into the tart forms, line with parchment paper and weigh down with beans or baking weights. Pre-bake the tart shells for 10 minutes in a hot oven.

2. Whisk the egg yolks, sugar, butter, fromage blanc, flour and raisins together in a bowl until smooth.

Blanc Cheesecake

3. In a separate bowl, beat the egg whites into stiff peaks, then fold them into the fromage blanc mixture.

4. Spread the bottoms of the tart shells with the guava jam. Spoon or pipe the fromage blanc mixture into the tarts and bake for 20 minutes at 400 °F/200 °C until brown and set. Serve immediately.

Citrus

For 20 tarts:
7 oz/200 g sweet pastry (see
   basic recipes)

For the lime tarts:
zest and juice of 2 limes
2 tbsp butter
½ cup plus 2 tbsp/150 g sugar
5 eggs

For the clementine tarts:
2 clementines
½ cup/120 ml whipping cream
1 tbsp/10 g chopped pistachios

For the grapefruit tarts:
1 grapefruit
3½ tbsp/50 ml white rum
½ cup/120 ml pastry cream (see
   basic recipe)

Serves	*4*
Preparation time:	*45 minutes*
Resting time:	*30 minutes*
Cooking time:	*10 minutes*
Difficulty:	★ ★

Refreshing tropical citrus! Pleasantly tart and very rich in vitamin C and potassium, fresh citrus fruits are used to make these colorful tarts.

A word of advice: When making the sweet pastry tart shells, do not knead the dough or work it too long because this will increase its elasticity, making it harder to roll and causing the baked shells to be tough and chewy.

The sweet pastry must be allowed to rest before it is rolled out to keep the sides of the tart shells from shrinking and falling when baked. Wrap the dough tightly in plastic wrap and set it aside for at least two hours in a cool dry place—or you may

store it for up to four days in the refrigerator. After the pastry has been rolled out, it should be allowed to rest a second time before being pressed into the tart shells. Finally, remember to use metal rather than glass or porcelain tart molds to bake the shells, since porcelain does not conduct heat as well as metal.

When making the lime tarts, allow the lime curd to cool before filling the tart shells. Garnish the tarts with a slice of lime or a lightly broiled meringue.

Serve these citrus tarts with a glass of champagne for a brilliant finale to a summer meal.

1. Roll out the sweet pastry and let it rest in the refrigerator for 2 hours. Using a round cutter slightly larger than the tart molds, cut rounds of dough for the shells. Press the pastry into the tart molds and bake for 5 minutes at 350 °F/180 °C.

2. To make the lime curd, peel the zest and sqeeze the limes. Bring the juice and zest to a boil in a saucepan, and stir in the butter and sugar. Whisk the hot mixture into the eggs in a separate bowl. Return the curd to the saucepan and cook for 2 minutes until thick, then strain and allow the curd to cool.

Tarts

3. For the clementine tarts, slice each clementine segment in half and arrange to form a circle. Whip the cream, then pipe it into the tart shells. Garnish with the clementine circles and sprinkle with chopped pistachios. For the lime tarts, place a little lime curd in the tart shells and top with a thin slice of lime.

4. For the grapefruit tarts, peel and segment the grapefruit, removing all traces of pith or membrane. Cut each segment into thirds, flavor the pastry cream with rum and pipe it into the tart shells. Garnish with several slices of grapefruit.

Tropical Fruit

For 20 tarts:
¾ cup/200 g shortbread pastry
(see basic recipes)

For the kiwi tarts:
2 tbsp/30 ml whipping cream
2 kiwis
3½ tbsp/50 g pastry cream
(see basic recipe)

For the dragon fruit tarts:
3½ tbsp/50 g pastry cream
(see basic recipes)
½ tsp ground cinnamon
1 dragon fruit
2 kumquats

For the pineapple tarts:
2 tbsp/30 ml whipping cream
1 passion fruit
3½ tbsp/50 g pastry cream
(see basic recipes)
¼ pineapple

Serves   4
Preparation time: 45 minutes
Cooking time: 5 minutes
Difficulty: ★ ★

What an array of exotic fruit! Kiwi, pineapple, dragon fruit, kumquat—and if that is not enough, you may also use star fruit, guava, soursop, mango, mangosteen, papaya… Any number of combinations are possible in this recipe. According to availability, more traditional, western fruits may also be used to make the tarts. To accentuate the tropical fruit flavors, macerate the fruit in rum, litchi liqueur, passion fruit liqueur, Triple Sec, or other alcohol. Feel free to improvise and experiment with this basic recipe and to create other flavor combinations.

Whipped cream, fruit mousse or a Chiboust cream (see the glossary) are alternative fillings which allow you to vary the tart compositions. Make sure to flavor the fillings with spices which will complement the particular tropical fruits chosen for the tarts. The increasing use of unusual tropical spices indicates just how important exotic spices have become in pastry-making.

The shortbread pastry requires a certain amount of care: Do not over-work the dough, and allow it sufficient time to chill and rest. The resulting dough will then be tender and crisp, rather than tough and chewy. Bake the tart shells in a slow oven until they are a light golden brown.

1. Roll out the shortbread pastry and cut it into rounds the size of the molds. Press the dough into the molds, weigh it down with beans or smaller molds, and bake for 5 minutes at 350 °F/ 180 °C. Remove the weights and cool, then remove the tart shells from the molds by pressing your thumb on the bottom of the form.

2. For the dragon fruit tart, flavor the pastry cream with the cinnamon and pipe it into the tart shells. Place a slice of the dragon fruit on top of the pastry cream, glaze with a fruit jelly, if desired, and garnish with a slice of kumquat.

Tarts

3. For the pineapple tarts, whip the cream with the passion fruit pulp, fold the whipped cream into the pastry cream to make a Chiboust cream, and pipe this cream into the tart shells. Place a triangle of pineapple on top and garnish with a few passion fruit seeds.

4. For the kiwi tarts, fold the whipped cream into the pastry cream to make a Chiboust cream. Pipe this into the tart shells and spoon cubes of kiwi on top. Serve an assortment of tarts to each guest.

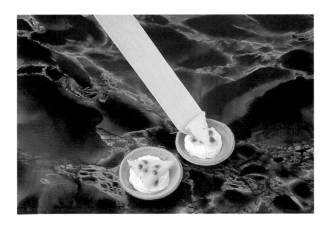

Banana Tarte Tatin

3½ tbsp/50 g butter
6½ tbsp/100 g sugar
4 baby bananas
4 rounds of puff pastry
   (see basic recipes)

For the piña colada sauce:
6½ tbsp/100 ml pineapple juice
6½ tbsp/100 ml coconut milk
6½ tbsp/100 ml aged dark rum

For the garnish:
several pomegranate seeds

Serves   4
Preparation time: 20 minutes
Cooking time: 25 minutes
Difficulty: ★ ★

The traditional *tarte tatin* is a tart which is baked upside down, with the fruit underneath the dough. The name comes form the famous Tatin sisters who, upon dropping the tart they were making while removing it from the oven, put it back together upside down.

Select firm baby bananas, which can be used whole. If these are not available, regular bananas sliced on a bias will also work in this recipe. Your tarte tatin may also be made with mangos, pears or apricots and served with your choice of sorbet.

Chef's hint: To allow the steam which accumulates as the fruit cooks to evaporate, make a small hole in the center of the puff pastry covering the fruit. Fresh or store-bought puff pastry may be used in this recipe. and sweet pastry (see basic recipe) also works well for the crust.

If the bananas have not caramelized sufficiently after the tart has been baked, sprinkle sugar over them and caramelize the top surface with a brûlée iron or the bottom of a blini pan heated on the stovetop.

Just before serving the Banana Tarte Tatin, warm the rum in a saucepan, pour it over the tart and flambée it. Heat the piña colada sauce and whip it in a blender until frothy. Garnish the plate with the warm sauce and several pomegranate seeds.

1. To prepare the butter caramel, melt the butter in individual metal pans, add the sugar and heat until a light caramel forms.

2. Lay the whole baby bananas directly into the hot syrup to caramelize them, then allow them to cool.

with Aged Rum

3. Cut rounds of puff pastry a little larger than the individual pans. Cover the cooled bananas with the dough, seal the edges and bake at 400 °F/200 °C for 20 minutes.

4. For the piña colada sauce, whisk together the pineapple juice, coconut milk and rum in a saucepan. Heat the mixture slightly, then blend it until frothy. Set each tarte tatin on a serving plate, garnish with the warm piña colada sauce and several pomegranate seeds, and serve hot.

Fruit and

For the hazelnut mousse:
¾ cup/100 g chopped hazelnuts
¾ cup/175 g butter, softened
⅔ cup/100 g confectioners' sugar
3½ tbsp/50 ml Triple Sec
½ cup/125 ml whipping cream

1 pint/250 g strawberries
3 kiwis
½ large mango

For the génoise:
 (see basic recipe)
2 cups plus 1½ tbsp/260 g flour
1 cup plus 1 tbsp/260 g sugar
½ cup/120 g butter
4 eggs
5 egg yolks

Serves	4
Preparation time:	50 minutes
Chilling time:	4 hours
Freezing time:	1 hour
Difficulty:	★ ★ ★

This original combination of orange-flavored Triple Sec and hazelnuts makes for a light, tasty mousse that provides a cohesive base for the diverse fruits in this dessert.

Prepare the cream carefully: The hazelnut and butter mixture must be at room temperature so that the addition of the cold whipped cream does not cause the butter to clot. No gelatin is used in this recipe in order to keep the mousse light and smooth.

When selecting the fruits, choose very ripe mangos which are not too soft, medium-sized kiwis, and large, red strawberries. Slice the fruit into quarters ahead of time. If mangos are not available, ripe, yellow peaches may also be used.

Freeze the génoise for thirty minutes before using to keep it from tearing and crumbling. For easier unmolding, line the terrine or loaf pan with aluminum foil before assembling the génoise shell.

Fill the terrine with three layers of fruit and mousse. Using the palm of your hand, press the fruit lightly into the mousse to eliminate any space or air. Alternate colors of fruit to create a mosaic effect when the terrine is sliced and served. This dessert may also be accompanied by your choice of fruit coulis.

1. To make the hazelnut mousse, beat together the chopped hazelnuts, softened butter, sugar and Triple Sec. Whip the cream to stiff peaks then fold it gently into the hazelnut mixture.

2. Wash and stem the strawberries and peel the other fruit. Cut the mangos and kiwis into quarters lengthwise.

Hazelnut Terrine

3. Line the terrine mold with aluminum foil. Using a serrated knife, cut thin slices of the génoise to line the bottom and sides of the terrine. Alternatively, a terra cotta terrine or aluminum loaf pan may be used.

4. To assemble the terrine, alternate layers of hazelnut mousse and fruit, pressing the fruit lightly with your hand to eliminate any holes or air bubbles. Top with a fourth slice of génoise and refrigerate for at least 4 hours. Serve with your choice of fruit coulis.

Creole

For the sabayon:
8 egg yolks
¾ cup/200 ml dark rum
3½ tbsp/50 ml sugar syrup (see
    basic recipes)

8¾ oz/250 g mascarpone cheese
½ cup plus 1 tsp/50 g grated coconut
4 egg whites
3½ tbsp/50 g sugar

2 cups/250 ml whipping cream
2 cups/250 ml coffee
8 slices génoise (see basic recipe)

For the decoration:
3½ tbsp/50 ml coconut milk
¼ cup unsweetened cocoa

Serves	*4*
Preparation time:	*45 minutes*
Cooking time:	*20 minutes*
Chilling time:	*4 hours*
Difficulty:	★ ★

Tiramisu has grown so popular as a dessert in recent years that it seems almost pointless to provide a recipe here. We have done so, however, in order to demonstrate what a true tiramisu is and disprove those who call any coffee-flavored cake by that name.

The contrast between the sweetness of the génoise and the bitter flavors of the coffee and cocoa is what makes this dessert so special. Select ingredients which are rich in flavor to accentuate the contrast.

A génoise cake has been chosen for this dessert for its capacity to absorb a maximum of liquid and still hold its shape when placed in the mold. Our chef recommends preparing the génoise a few days ahead of time so that it is slightly dry and stale and will not crumble or fall apart when soaked.

If you are making this dessert at home, you can ease your task by using a different mold from the one shown here; but if you do opt for pyramid molds, lightly moisten the parchment triangles used to line the molds to make them to adhere to the sides of the pyramid. Make sure there are no creases or bubbles between the paper and the mold.

Here is our chef's hint for the sabayon: Cook the sabayon, whisking constantly, until you can see the trail of the whisk drawn distinctly in the mousse. When you can see the outline of the whisk, the correct consistency has been obtained and the sabayon is ready.

1. Prepare a sabayon with the egg yolks, 3½ tbsp/50 ml of the rum and the sugar syrup. Whisking constantly, warm the mixture over low heat until thick and frothy, then allow to cool.

2. Whisk the mascarpone cheese until smooth, then fold it into the sabayon and add the grated coconut. Beat the eggs with the sugar until stiff peaks form, then whip the cream and fold the egg whites and the whipped cream into the sabayon.

Tiramisu

3. Brew 2 cups of very strong coffee and add the rest of the rum to it. Trim the edges of the génoise and cut it into 5 squares to fit the base of the molds. Cut 1 of the 5 slices into quarters and soak all of the génoise pieces in the coffee.

4. Line the sides of each pyramid mold with 4 triangles of parchment paper. Fill the tip of the mold with the mascarpone mixture. Press 1 of the smaller quarters of génoise into the mascarpone, fill the rest of the mold with the mixture, and close with a whole slice of génoise. Chill for at least 4 hours. Unmold, sprinkle with cocoa powder and serve, garnished with coconut milk and cocoa powder.

Chocolatine Napoleon

For the nougatine:
½ cup plus 2 tbsp/150 g sugar
2 tbsp water
½ cup plus 1 tbsp/70 g chopped hazelnuts
½ cup plus 1 tbsp/70 g chopped almonds
3½ oz/100 g dark chocolate

For the ganache:
¾ cup/200 ml whipping cream
1 tbsp spiced Christmas tea
7 oz/200 g dark chocolate

For the custard: (see basic recipes)
3 egg yolks
3½ tbsp/50 g sugar
1 cup/250 ml milk

Serves   4
Preparation time: 30 minutes
Cooking time: 20 minutes
Difficulty: ★ ★

This elegant treat is a guaranteed crowd-pleaser at Christmas dinner or any other festive occasion. The flavors of the dark chocolate and the nougatine are enhanced by the incomparable spicy flavor of Christmas tea.

Tea is the most popular beverage in the world next to water. There are countless types of tea: India Darjeeling and Chinese Oolong are just two of the best known varieties. In this recipe, we have chosen to use Christmas tea, a British favorite during the winter months, because it unites the strong flavor of flat-leafed, semi-fermented black tea with the potent spices carried back to Britain from India along Spice Route: cloves, cinnamon and orange zest. The distinctive flavor of this tea also balances out the sweetness of the nougatine.

The only tricky maneuver in making this dessert is adding the chocolate to the hot nougatine without burning it. Once the nougatine has caramelized, allow it to cool for a few minutes before stirring in the melted chocolate.

For the ganache, our chef recommends steeping the tea in the cream as long as possible so that the cream absorbs a maximum of flavor. During this time, the cream should not be allowed to boil.

The chocolate nougatine may be made with pistachios or peanuts in place of the almonds and hazelnuts, if desired.

1. To make the nougatine, stir together the sugar and water in a saucepan, bring them to a boil and cook over high heat for 10 minutes until the caramel turns a light brown. Stir in the hazelnuts and almonds to make the nougatine.

2. While the nougatine is cooling, melt the dark chocolate and stir it carefully into the cooled nougatine. Spread the nougatine-chocolate mixture in a thin layer on a non-stick baking sheet and allow to cool, then break it into large, irregularly shaped pieces.

Flavored with Christmas Tea

3. To make the ganache, bring the cream to a boil in a saucepan, then remove it from the heat. Steep the Christmas tea in the cream for around 10 minutes. Melt the chocolate for the ganache.

4. Strain the tea-infused cream and pour it over the melted chocolate. Mix well and allow to cool. To assemble the desert, lay a piece of nougatine on the plate, pipe the ganache on top and repeat, stacking the nougatine on top of the ganache. Finish with a piece of nougatine. Garnish the plate with the custard, if desired, and serve.

Madinina

For the banana mousse:
8¾ oz/250 g bananas
6 sheets of gelatin
2 tbsp/30 g sugar
3½ tbsp/50 ml rum
1 whole nutmeg, grated
⅔ cup/150 ml whipping cream

For the coconut mousse:
6½ tbsp/100 ml coconut milk
4 sheets gelatin

⅓ cup/30 g gated coconut
2 tbsp/30 g sugar
3½ tbsp/50 ml Malibu coconut liqueur
1⅔ cup/400 ml whipping cream

For the chocolate mousse:
5¼ oz/150 g dark chocolate
⅔ cup/150 ml whipping cream
1 sheet gelatin

Serves	*4*
Preparation time:	*1 hour 30 minutes*
Cooking time:	*15 minutes*
Chilling time:	*3 hours*
Difficulty:	*0★ ★*

This delicate dessert unites three traditional tropical flavors: banana, coconut and chocolate. The dark chocolate mousse (milk chocolate may also be used), adds character and contrast to the sweetness of the banana and coconut. To insure a perfect balance of flavors, maintain the proportions given in the recipes and select high-quality ingredients.

For the sake of simplifying the preparation, this mousse trio may be reduced to a duo by incorporating the chocolate mousse into either the banana or the coconut mousse.

When making the mousses, soften the gelatin sheets in cold water before adding them to the mixtures. If you do not have gelatin sheets, fold whipped egg whites into the mousses to add stability and smoothness.

Special care must be taken to spread each layer of mousse evenly in order to preserve their distinctness when unmolded. We leave the decoration of this dessert up to you: Here, we have used chocolate shavings, grated coconut and chocolate sauce for the garnish. Other possibilities include an espresso sauce, a banana-rum coulis or a vanilla custard.

1. For the banana mousse, peel and purée the bananas. Soften the gelatin and soften it by placing it in the microwave for a few seconds on high. Stir the gelatin, sugar, rum and a pinch of freshly-grated nutmeg into the banana purée. Whip the cream into stiff peaks and fold it into the banana mixture. Spread a layer of the mousse in each mold and refrigerate for 1 hour.

2. Follow the same steps for the coconut mousse as for the banana mousse, eliminating the nutmeg and replacing the rum with the Malibu liqueur. Fill the molds two-thirds full with a layer of the coconut mousse and refrigerate for 1 hour.

Mousse Trio

3. For the chocolate mousse, melt the dark chocolate and whip the cream. Soften the gelatin as described in Step 1 and stir it into the warm chocolate until completely dissolved, then fold in the whipped cream. Spoon a layer of chocolate mousse into each mold and refrigerate 1 hour.

4. Unmold the mousse trio using a thin knife. If desired, prepare a chocolate sauce to garnish the plate by melting 1 oz/30 g dark chocolate in a double boiler. Sprinkle with coconut and chocolate shavings and serve.

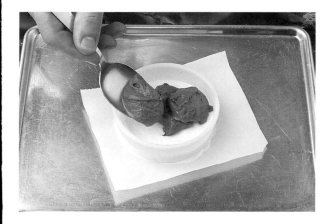

Ginger and

6½ tbsp/100 g flour
¾ cup plus 1 tbsp/200 g sugar
1⅔ cup/200 g slivered almonds
1 cup/250 ml lime juice
6½ tbsp/100 g butter, melted
2 egg whites
1 heaping tsp/10 g fresh grated ginger

Serves	4
Preparation time:	15 minutes
Cooking time:	15 minutes
Chilling time:	overnight
Difficulty:	★ ★

A smooth, brown-skinned root with a strong and spicy flavor, ginger was first imported to the West in the days of the British Empire. According to Chinese tradition, the digestive qualities of ginger are best put to use when it is eaten, fresh or candied, at the end of a meal.

The slivered almonds called for in this recipe may be replaced by chopped almonds, walnuts, pecans or hazelnuts. The lime-ginger combination contributes a pleasant sweet-and-sour flavor to these almond tuiles. Orange or lemon zest may also be substituted for the lime.

Check the tuiles regularly while they are baking to insure that they brown evenly. They should be a dark golden brown when served. Once the tuiles are removed from the oven, lay them flat or shape them as we have done here into crisp, curved cookies. To form the tuiles, lay them on a curved pan or bend them around a rolling pin while they are still warm and flexible. Once cooled, they become crisp and cannot be formed. You may even out the edges by trimming them with scissors or a cookie cutter while they are still hot.

Serve these ginger-lime tuiles to accompany a lemon, orange or grapefruit sorbet or perhaps just a glass of champagne served at the end of a meal.

1. Stir together the flour, sugar, almonds, lime juice, melted butter and egg whites.

2. Add the grated ginger to the mixture and refrigerate the batter overnight.

Lime Tuiles

3. Using a spoon, spread the batter into circles on a non-stick baking sheet. Bake the tuiles for 15 minutes at 320 °F/160 °C.

4. Remove the tuiles from the oven and cool slightly. While the tuiles are still warm, shape them around a rolling pin and cool completely. Store in air-tight containers until they are served.

Caribbean

For the tulip batter:
6½ tbsp butter, melted
¾ cup/120 g confectioners' sugar
¾ cup plus 1 tbsp/100 g flour
3 egg whites
¼ cup chopped pistachios

2 clementines
2 kiwis
2 mandarin oranges
1 pineapple
1 grapefruit
¾ cup plus 1 tbsp/200 g sugar

Serves	4
Preparation time:	*20 minutes*
Cooking time:	*20 minutes*
Chilling time:	*10 minutes*
Resting Time:	*24 hours*
Difficulty:	★

The thin, crunchy sugar shell which coats the fruit in this recipe is made by dipping the fruit in sugar which has reached the hard ball stage, meaning that a droplet of the sugar can be shaped by hand into a hard, breakable ball which does not stick to your fingers. The temperature of the sugar is essential: If it is too hot, it turns to caramel, but sugar which is not hot enough fails to coat the fruit correctly and sticks to the teeth.

Each stage of cooked sugar has a different use. It requires practice to test the sugar with your fingers, but here is one way to do it: Drop a spoonful of the heated sugar into a glass of ice water, then attempt to roll it between your thumb and index finger to test its consistency.

Slice the fruit and dry it on a clean towel before dipping it in the sugar. When segmenting the citrus fruits, leave the thin membrane which surrounds the juicy pulp on the fruit. Oranges, pink grapefruit or pomelos may also be used in this recipe.

Our chef recommends shaping the tuiles while hot to keep them from breaking. If the tulips cool and harden too quickly, reheat them for a minute or two in the oven to soften them once more in order to shape them.

This delicious, refreshing dessert of fruit nestled inside a crisp tulip shell is perfect after a light summer meal. Garnish with pomegranate seeds for added color and effect.

1. To make the tulip batter, melt the butter in a saucepan, add the confectioners' sugar and flour, then stir in the egg whites. Spread the batter in extremely thin circles on non-stick baking sheets and refrigerate them overnight.

2. Sprinkle the tulips with the chopped pistachios and bake for 5 to 6 minutes at 400 °F/ 200 °C. Remove the tulips from the oven and carefully raise them from the baking sheet with a spatula. Press each hot circle into a bowl (or drape over an overturned bowl) to shape like a tulip and allow to cool.

Fruit Tulip

3. In a saucepan, bring the sugar and water to a boil and cook the syrup to the hard ball stage (300 °F/145–150 °C) to make the sugar coating for the fruit.

4. Slice and segment the fruit. Dip each piece of fruit into the hot sugar syrup and drain on a non-stick baking sheet. Once the fruit has cooled, fill the tulip shells, alternating colors and shapes, and serve.

Tiger-Banana

4 vanilla beans
2 cups/500 ml milk
2 cups/500 ml whipping cream
4 bananas

12 egg yolks
1 cup/250 g sugar
3½ tbsp/50 g butter
1 tbsp/15 g raw sugar

Serves	*4*
Preparation time:	*35 minutes*
Cooking time:	*2 hours*
Chilling time:	*1 hour 30 minutes*
Difficulty:	★

Bananas are picked while still green and then stored in a special room until they ripen and are ready to be sold commercially. Available year-round, ripe bananas are bright yellow with black striations. For this custard, select firm, ripe bananas with a lot of flavor.

Look for so-called "Bourbon" or Tahitian vanilla beans to flavor the milk and cream. Cut each bean lengthwise and scrape the seeds into a saucepan containing the milk and cream. Bring the milk to a boil and let the vanilla steep as long as possible. Remove the vanilla beans before making the custard. The vanilla beans can be reused by grinding them in the blender to make powdered vanilla.

The individual custards are poached in the oven in a pan of simmering water until set. Our chef recommends laying a piece of parchment paper on top of the water to keep it from splashing into the ramekins of custard as they bake.

Canned pears in syrup may be replace the bananas in this recipe. The cream mixture may also be infused with walnuts or other dried fruits for flavor. To make a crunchy sugar topping, sprinkle the baked custards with raw sugar and place under the broiler for several minutes.

1. Cut each vanilla bean lengthwise and scrape the seeds into a saucepan containing the milk and cream. Simmer over low heat for 30 minutes.

2. Slice the bananas lengthwise. Beat the eggs and sugar together to ribbon consistency in a bowl. Pour the cream mixture over the eggs, whisking constantly. Chill the mixture.

Vahine Custard

3. Prepare a caramel with the butter and raw sugar. Caramelize the bananas in the syrup and allow to cool.

4. Line each ramekin with the caramelized bananas, leaving no space between the slices. Pour the custard over the bananas to the top of the molds, then place the filled ramekins in a pan of simmering water in the oven and poach for about 2 hours at 275 °F/ 140 °C until set. Serve cold.

Glossary

ALMOND FLOUR: Blanched almonds which have been ground to a powder. Almond flour is sold commercially or can be made by chopping blanched almonds in a food processor until they have a powdery consistancy.

APRICOT GLAZE: Hot, strained apricot jam can be spread onto pastries, either as a glaze or as an isolating layer between cake and moist cream or fruit fillings.

BAIN-MARIE: Also called water bath, a gentle method of heating used to either cook food or keep food warm, a bain-marie consists of a pan containing food placed inside a larger pan of warm (not boiling) water, surrounding the smaller pan with heat. Placed in an oven, a bain-marie generates steam for foods that require moister heat than that generated by home ovens.

BISCUIT: The French word for sponge cake.

TO BLANCH: Briefly immersing foods in boiling water and then immediately in cold water to stop the cooking. This process makes it easier to remove peels and skins, rids food of impurities, and preserves the flavor and color of food before freezing.

BLINI PAN: A small cast iron pan approximately 5 in/13 cm in diameter with a thick bottom and high sides which is used to make blinis. Blini pans are also used to caramelize the tops of custards by heating the pan and placing it directly on a sugared surface.

BLINIS OR BLINTZES: Small savory pancakes made with white and buckwheat flour and leavened with yeast.

BRICK PASTRY: see *Feuille de brick*.

BRIOCHE: A classic French yeast bread, very light, yet made rich by eggs and butter.

CARAMEL: Caramel is produced when sugar is heated to 320-350 °F/160-177 °C and becomes light to dark brown. Other ingredients like water, cream and butter are added to the caramel to make sauces or candies, but liquid must be added carefully and gradually to sugar heated to these temperatures!

TO CARAMELIZE: To heat sugar until it becomes caramel (see above); or to coat something with caramel syrup; or to sprinkle sugar on the surface of a dessert and then broil or grill it briefly until the sugar turns into caramel (for example, a crème brûlée).

CHANTILLY: A term from French culinary vocabulary, *à la chantilly* means that a dish, sweet or savory, is served with or incorporates whipped cream. Crème chantilly is simply whipped cream, most often lightly sweetened with vanilla, sugar or liqueurs.

CHOUX PASTRY: A simple but unique dough that is prepared on the stovetop by bringing water or milk to a boil, adding flour and then stirring in several eggs to form a sticky paste. This is the classic cream puff pastry.

CLARIFIED BUTTER: Butter that has been melted slowly without stirring, then skimmed and decanted, leaving the milk solids and water in the pan. This liquid is pure butter fat and has a higher smoking point than whole butter, but less intense buttery flavor.

TO CLARIFY: To remove any particles which interfere with the clear appearance of liquids (i.e. jelly or consommé), usually by straining or binding the impurities, often by adding and then straining out egg white.

TO COAT: In baking, coating refers to covering the surface of cakes and pastries with a thin layer often of chocolate or marzipan.

CONFECTIONERS' SUGAR: American term for icing sugar, also known as powdered sugar.

COULIS: A thick sauce consisting primarily of puréed fruit, occasionally with lemon juice, sugar or other ingredients added to enhance its flavor.

CRÈME FRAÎCHE: A thickened cream with an incomparably smooth texture and nutty, not sour, taste. If not readily available, crème fraîche can be simulated by adding 1 tsp–1 tbsp buttermilk to 1 cup heavy cream and letting the mixture stand at room temperature 8–24 hours until thickened. This will keep up to 10 days in the refrigerator.

TO DEGLAZE: To use a liquid such as water, fruit juice, alcohol or stock to dissolve food particles remaining in a pan after food has been sautéed in it. This liquid is normally used as the basis of a sauce.

TO DICE: To cut fruit or vegetables into even, dice-like shapes. Traditionally, dice is about ¼–½ in/5 mm in size.

DOUBLE BOILER: A double boiler consists of two pans that nestle into each other. The bottom pan is filled with simmering water and the top pan rests over, but not in, the hot water, providing the gentle heat necessary to melt or cook delicate foods like custards or sauces. Compare to bain-marie.

FEUILLE DE BRICK: A paper-thin crêpe made with boiled semolina flour. Feuille de brick are made by spreading a thin layer of semolina dough onto a hot griddle and removing it almost immediately, before it browns. Feuille de brick are used for crispy outer casings of desserts in place of phyllo dough or puff pastry.

FEUILLETÉ: A French word meaning "flaky" and often used to refer to pastries which are made with rich, many-layered puff pastry. See also *Millefeuille*.

TO FLAMBÉ: To pour alcohol over food and light the alcohol, imparting a very special flavor. This can be a dramatic presentation or an earlier step in the cooking process.

TO FLOUR: Also called dusting, this means coating a greased baking pan with a very fine layer of flour so that the item baked in it can be more easily removed. Other ingredients can be used instead of flour including, for example, sugar, bread crumbs, sesame seeds, or finely ground almonds.

TO FOLD: Also to blend; a means of combining two mixtures of varying densities (for example, egg whites and custard). With the lighter mass on top of the heavier one, use a spatula to cut through both, scrape along the bottom of the bowl, and up the side. Continue this, rotating the bowl slightly with each stroke. Folding must be done carefully, gently, and yet rapidly to retain the volume of the lighter mixture.

FRANGIPANE: A variation of pastry cream that is usually flavored with ground almonds and used in various cakes and pastries.

FROMAGE BLANC: A mild fresh cheese similar to cottage cheese in flavor, but not in texture. Fromage blanc has a silky, smooth texture like that of sour cream.

GANACHE: An extraordinary, rich chocolate cream made by heating whipping cream and allowing chocolate to melt in it. Depending on its texture, ganache can be used as a coating, filling, or sauce.

TO GARNISH: Decorating a dish to make it more visually appealing with various edible elements; also refers to the decoration itself. Garnish varies from a single sprig of mint, to the additions to a soup, to entire side dishes.

GELATIN: A clear and flavorless substance used to jell liquid mixtures. Gelatin is available in ¼ oz/7 g envelopes of granules (more common in North America) and in paper-thin sheets or leaves (standard in Europe). Leaf gelatin should be soaked in cold water for 5–10 minutes, then thoroughly wrung out before, like ground gelatin, being dissolved in a small amount of hot liquid before use. One envelope of granules or 4 leaves of gelatin is generally sufficient to jell 2 cups/500 ml liquid.

GÉNOISE: A variation of sponge cake, in which whole eggs are beaten with sugar to the ribbon stage (see ribbon stage) before flour, finely-ground nuts, or other ingredients are folded in.

GLACÉ: A French term meaning chilled, iced or frozen.

TO GLAZE: To spread a thin layer of eggs, jelly or jam, gum arabic, or any other kind of coating onto foods to give them a shiny finish.

TO GREASE OR BUTTER: Brushing a thin layer of butter or some other fat onto baking pans so that the finished product can be removed from the pans without tearing.

HEAVY CREAM: This is the American term for double cream.

HOT OVEN: 400–425 °F or 205–220 °C

TO INFUSE: see to steep

INSTANT CUSTARD MIX: Unsweetened instant custard mix, also called *"poudre à flan."* Bird's English Custard Mix is one brand available on the market.

ITALIAN MERINGUE: A variation of meringue made by pouring hot sugar syrup over whipped egg whites while beating continuously until the mixture has cooled completely.

TO KNEAD: To thoroughly combine and work the components of a dough either by hand or with the dough hook of an electric mixer to produce a homogenous dough. It can take 15 minutes or longer to produce a smooth, elastic dough when kneading by hand.

LIGHT CREAM: This is the American term for single cream.

TO LINE: To cover the inside of a mold or pan with whatever ingredient is called for. For a charlotte, ladyfingers would be used. For aspic, the mold would be lined with gelatin.

LOW OVEN: 300–325 °F or 150–165 °C

TO MACERATE/MARINATE: To soak foods in an aromatic liquid (marinade) for a period of time to allow the food to take on the flavor of the liquid and become more tender. Fruits soaked in liqueur are macerated; meat or fish in a savory liquid is marinated.

MELON BALLER: A special spoon shaped like a tiny bowl used to carve circles from melons and other fruits and vegetables.

MERINGUE: A light mass of stiffly beaten egg whites, often sweetened with sugar, which can be used as an icing or topping, an element of a mousse, cream or soufflé, or baked as cookies or bases for gâteaux. See also Italian meringue.

MILLEFEUILLE: The French word literally means "thousand leaves" and refers to the multitude of buttery-light layers in perfect puff pastry. Mille-feuille is also a 3-tiered sweet consisting of puff pastry filled with cream, custard or fruit and dusted with confectioners' sugar or glazed on top. The classic version, with pastry cream, is known as a Napoleon in North America, or vanilla slice in Britain.

MODERATE OVEN: 350–375 °F or 175–190 °C

PÂTE: The French word for many kinds of mixtures in baking, including dough, batter and pastry. Short pastry is *pâte brisée*, short sweet pastry is *pâte sucrée*, crêpe batter is *pâte à crêpe*, and so forth.

TO POACH: A method of cooking food by immersing it in hot, but not boiling, water or other liquid.

TO PREBAKE: To bake a pie crust or pastry shell without a filling. Prick the pastry with fork and weight it down with dried beans or baking beans so it does not rise or contort while baking.

TO PURÉE: To blend or mash food until it has a perfectly smooth consistency, often by means of a blender or food processor. Purée also refers to the puréed food itself.

QUENELLE: An oval-shaped scoop of mousse, ice cream or any other unctuous ingredient shaped using two soup spoons.

TO RECONSTITUTE: To add liquid to dried or dehydrated foods, such as powdered milk or dried fruits and vegetables.

TO REFRESH: A means of preventing foods from continuing to cook in their own heat either by immersing the cooking pan in cold water or running cold water directly onto the food immediately after removing it from the heat.

RIBBON STAGE: When beating sugar with eggs, they should become pale yellow and reach the ribbon stage, so called because the mixture falls in silky ribbons from the whisk or beaters.

SABAYON: Also known by its Italian name, zabaglione, it is an extremely light, frothy custard consisting of egg yolks, sugar and wine or other spirits that are vigorously whisked over a gentle source of heat.

TO SAUTÉ: A method of cooking in a very small amount of hot oil or other fat, usually in an uncovered pan. Food may be lightly sautéed just to brown its surface, or cooked all the way through.

SPONGE CAKE: A classic sponge cake consists of egg whites and egg yolks, each beaten separately with sugar until light and foamy, then folded together and enriched with a little flour, ground nuts, or other ingredients. There are virtually infinite variations of sponge cakes, and they form the basis of a vast array of gâteaux and other desserts.

SPUN SUGAR: Thin filaments of cooked or caramelized sugar which are "spun" by drawing them across a flat, clean surface. Spun sugar can be gathered up to make nests, garlands or other decorations for desserts.

TO STEEP OR INFUSE: To soak an ingredient in a liquid, usually hot, for several minutes in order to impart its flavor to the liquid (for example, tea in hot water, or a vanilla bean in milk when making custard).

TO STRAIN: To pour or press ingredients through a sieve or a piece of cheesecloth in order to remove impurities, lumps, or seeds.

SUGAR SYRUP: A solution of sugar and water that have been boiled together. It is indispensable in baking and confection-making. The density of sugar syrup varies according to the proportions of sugar and water used; unless otherwise noted the recipes in this volume call for a heavy syrup made of equal parts sugar and water.

TO TEMPER: A method of preparing chocolate to be used for decorative work or coating by slowly melting it, then allowing it to partially cool, then reheating it very briefly. This complex process serves to prevent the cocoa butter contained in the chocolate from crystallizing, which would severely detract from the appearance of the finished product.

TUILE: Literally meaning "tile" in French, a tuile is a very thin wafer that is draped over an object or placed in a form while still warm and flexible, resulting in decorative cookies that can also be used as vessels for custard, mousse, etc.

VANILLA SUGAR: Sugar infused with the flavor of vanilla bean, or containing some ground vanilla. This can easily be made at home by placing one or more vanilla beans in a jar filled with sugar. After a week or two the sugar will be permeated with the aroma of vanilla.

VERY HOT OVEN: 450–475 °F or 230–245 °C

Basic Recipes

Sponge Cake

Ingredients:
6 eggs – 1 cup/250 g sugar – 2 cups/250 g flour – 3½ tbsp/50 g butter, melted

Preparation:
In a bowl, beat the eggs and sugar until they have reached the ribbon stage. Sift the flour over the bowl and fold it in with a wooden spoon. Blend in the melted butter.

Ladyfingers

Ingredients:
8 eggs, separated – 1 cup/250 g sugar – 1½ cup plus 2 tbsp/190 g flour – ½ tsp baking powder

Preparation:
Beat the egg yolks with 6½ tbsp/100 g sugar to ribbon consistency. In a separate bowl, whip the egg whites with the remaining sugar until firm. Fold the egg whites into the yolk mixture, then add the sifted flour and baking powder.

Crème Anglaise (custard)

Ingredients:
4 cups/1 liter milk – ¾ cup plus 1 tbsp/200 g sugar – 12 egg yolks – 1 vanilla bean

Preparation:
Add half the sugar and the vanilla bean to the milk and bring to a boil. In a small bowl, whisk the egg yolks with the remaining sugar. Add a few tablespoons of hot milk to the yolks, beating constantly. Pour the yolk mixture into the saucepan and cook until thick, stirring continuously with a wooden spoon and without allowing the mixture to boil. Remove from heat and continue stirring until completely cooled. Strain, if desired.

Orange Crème Anglaise (custard)

Ingredients:
2 cups/500 ml milk – 3½ tbsp/50 g sugar – 3 egg yolks – ¾ cup/200 ml orange juice concentrate

Preparation:
Follow the directions for the crème anglaise above, adding the orange juice concentrate once the custard has thickened.

Candied Lemons

Ingredients:
4 lemons, quartered – 3½ tbsp/50 ml water – ½ tsp sugar – ½ vanilla bean – ½ star anise – several crushed peppercorns

Preparation:
Quarter the lemons and blanch them in 3 changes of water. In a saucepan, combine the water, sugar, vanilla, star anise and peppercorns and bring to a boil. Add the blanched lemon and simmer over low heat for 1½ to 2 hours. Let the lemons cool in the liquid overnight and then drain.

Pastry Cream

Ingredients:
12 eggs – ¾ cup plus 1 tbsp/200 g sugar – 1 cup/120 g flour – 4 cups/1 liter milk – 1 vanilla bean – a pinch of salt

Preparation:
In a bowl, thoroughly beat the eggs and sugar. Whisk in the flour and 6½ tbsp/100 ml of the milk to keep the pastry cream smooth. In a saucepan, bring the rest of the milk to a boil with the vanilla bean and salt. Pour the boiling milk over the egg mixture, whisking constantly. Return the cream to the pan and boil for 3 minutes, stirring the entire time, until thickened. Cool and refrigerate until needed.

Whipped Cream

Ingredients:
2 cups/500 ml heavy cream – 1⅔ cups/200 g confectioners' sugar – 1 tsp vanilla extract

Preparation:
Whip the chilled cream until soft peaks form. Gradually add the sugar and continue beating until firm. Stir in vanilla extract to flavor and refrigerate until needed.

Puff Pastry

Ingredients:
3⅓ cups/400 g flour – ¾ tsp/8 g salt – ⅔ cup/150 ml water – 2½ cups/600 g butter*

Preparation:
Make a well in the flour on a clean work surface. Melt 13 tbsp/200 g of the butter and pour it into the well with the salt and water. Mix the flour and liquid and roll the dough into a ball without kneading. Refrigerate the dough for 20 minutes, then roll it out into a square on the work surface. Soften the remaining butter and place it on the square. Fold the 4 corners of the square over the butter. This is one "turn." Make 2 turns, refrigerating the pastry for 20 minutes in between, a total of 3 times.

* In hot climates and in tropical regions, butter should be substituted with adequate puff pastry shortening, which can be found in most grocery stores.

Génoise

Ingredients:
6 eggs (300 g) – 5 egg yolks (100 g) – 1 cup plus 2 tbsp/260 g sugar – 2 cups plus 2 tbsp/260 g flour – ½ cup/120 g butter

Preparation:
In a double boiler over low heat (98 °F/37 °C), whisk the eggs, egg yolks and sugar to ribbon consistency. Using a wooden spoon, fold in the sifted flour and finally the melted butter. Bake for 20 minutes at 350 °F/170 °C.

Vanilla Ice Cream

Ingredients:
4 cups/1 liter milk – 10 vanilla beans – ¾ cup plus 1 tbsp/200 g sugar – 12 egg yolks – ½ cup/125 ml crème fraîche

Preparation:
Boil the milk with the vanilla beans and half the sugar. In the top of a double boiler, combine the egg yolks and remaining sugar. Warm the yolk mixture by whisking in a small amount of boiling milk, then return all the custard to the saucepan and cook over low heat until it coats the back of a wooden spoon. Whisk in the crème fraîche, cool completely, and process in an ice cream maker.

Choux Pastry

Ingredients:
1 cup/250 ml milk – 1 tsp/5 g salt – 1 tsp/5g sugar – 6½ tbsp/100 g butter – 1¼ cups/150 g flour – 4 large eggs

Preparation:
In a pot, bring the milk to a boil with the salt, sugar, and butter, sliced into small pieces. As soon as the butter has melted, remove from the heat, add the flour and stir vigorously with a wooden spoon until a homogenous paste forms. Dry the dough by cooking over very low heat for about 10 minutes, stirring continuously. The pastry should pull away from the sides of the pot. When it no longer sticks to the spoon, remove from heat. Stir in the eggs with a wooden spoon, one by one, incorporating them well.

Crêpe Batter

Ingredients:
2 cups/250 g flour, sifted – 6 eggs – 2 cups/500 ml milk – 1 cup/250 ml heavy cream – 2 tbsp Grand Marnier – 1 tsp vanilla extract – ¼ cup/60 g butter

Preparation:
Form a well in the flour and break in the eggs. Combine the eggs and flour without allowing lumps to form. Add the milk, cream, Grand Marnier and vanilla extract. Slice the butter, add it to the batter and stir it in as well as possible. Refrigerate the batter 2–3 hours or overnight-before proceeding as directed in the recipe.

Pâte Brisée – Short Butter Pastry

Ingredients:
¼ cup/30 g confectioners' sugar – 1 egg yolk – a pinch of salt – ¼ cup /60 g butter – half a vanilla bean – ¾ cup/90 g flour

Preparation:
In a food processor, combine all the ingredients except the flour until they are well-blended and have a smooth texture. Gradually add the flour and mix thoroughly. Wrap the pastry in a cloth and refrigerate it overnight, if possible, because this makes the pastry much easier to work with.

Shortbread Pastry

Ingredients:
2 cups/250 g flour – ½ cup plus 2 tbsp confectioners' sugar – a pinch of salt – a pinch of baking powder – zest of 1 lemon – ½ cup plus 2 tbsp/150 g butter, softened – 1 egg

Preparation:
Combine thoroughly the flour, confectioners' sugar, salt, baking powder and lemon zest. Rub the butter into the dry ingredients with your fingers. Mix in the egg until the pastry forms a ball, but do not knead. Wrap the pastry in a cloth and refrigerate overnight before proceeding.

Sweet Pastry

Ingredients:
1½ cups/350 g butter, softened – ½ cup/125 g confectioners' sugar – ¼ cup/60 g sugar – ½ cup/65 g almond flour – 5 cups/625 g flour – 3 eggs

Preparation:
Combine the butter, confectioners' sugar, sugar, almond flour, and 1 cup/125 g of the flour. Stir in the eggs and remaining flour. Mix the dough together with your hands until smooth. Refrigerate, preferably overnight, before proceeding.

Piña Colada Sauce

Ingredients:
¾ cup/200 ml coconut milk – 2 cups/ 500 ml pineapple juice – ¾ cup/ 200 ml rum – ¾ cup/200 ml sugar syrup (see basic recipe below)

Preparation:
Blend all the ingredients together and proceed as directed.

Sugar Syrup

Ingredients:
4 cups/1 liter water – 4 cups/1 kg sugar

Preparation:
Dissolve the sugar in the water and let it boil for 3 minutes.

Index of Recipes